Poems for a Liminal Age

To Pat –
Miles Salter
x

With best wishes,
Simon Zonenblick, Nov 15

Every good with

Ian McEvoy Nov 2015

very Best Wishes

x

To Pat with every good wish.

2015.

G000163258

SPM
Publications

London

SPM Publications
Unit 136, 113-115 George Lane, South Woodford,
London E18 1AB, United Kingdom
www.spmpublications.com
www.sentinelwriting.com

First published in Great Britain by SPM Publications – an imprint of
Sentinel Writing & Publishing Company Limited in August 2015.

ISBN 978-0-9927055-6-5

Edited by Mandy Pannett
Book & cover design by Nnorom Azuonye
Cover background image courtesy of Microsoft Publisher clipart.
Set in Palatino

Poems for a Liminal Age

Edited by

Mandy Pannett

Acknowledgments

The publisher and editor of *Poems for a Liminal Age* are grateful for the generosity of the poets who have freely given their work for use in this anthology published in aid of Médecins Sans Frontières (Doctors Without Borders).

Special thanks go to the publishers and editors of books, journals, websites and blogs in which some of the poems in this book have previously appeared.

Afam Akeh selections from 'Endnotes' appears on the Centre for African Poetry website www.centreforafricanpoetry.org

Roselle Angwin 'Midwinter Solstice' previously appeared on her blog: 'qualia & other wildlife' (http://roselle-angwin.blogspot.co.uk)

Nnorom Azuonye 'Postcards from London' published in 'African Writing' 2008

S. M Beckett 'Winter in Caroni' was published in *Caught in the Net* December 2014

Linda Black 'Says the Onlooker' and 'Somewhere a Shelf' are from *Root* (Shearsman)

Peter Branson 'Ghosts' was first published in *Agenda*

Lesley Burt 'Your Child' was first published online by *Long Exposure* Oct 2014

Judith Cair 'The Lock at Flatford' and 'Topped' were first published in *The Ship's Eye* (Pighog Press 2012)

Michael Cantor 'The Journalist' was originally published in *The Dark Horse* in 2007, and also appeared in the author's collection, *Life in the Second Circle* (Able Muse Press, 2012.)

Jeff Cloves 'Gardens of Earthly Delight' was published in *Landmarks* (Ourside Stroud, 2014)

Rachael Clyne 'Dodgy Leads' Published in *Sarasvati Magazine* 2014 (Indigo Dreams)

Anna Crowe 'Hinterland' was commissioned by the Edinburgh Royal College of Surgeons to celebrate their quincentenary, and published in *The Hand that Sees*, (Scottish Poetry Library)

Chris O'Carroll 'Habitat' was originally published in *Angle*

Caroline Davies 'Ambush' was published by the Royal Academy of Arts in 2014.

Martin Elster 'The Loneliest Road' originally appeared in *cahoodaloodaling*

Joe Fearn 'News Report from a Northern Town' was published by Smith Doorstop 2012

Rachel J. Fenton 'Outliers' was published in the Shorelines issue of *JAAM*

John Freeman 'The Pond in the Fields' and 'It Was Us' were first published in *Envoi 161*

Caron Freeborn 'Theme Park' is published in her poetry collection *Georges Perec is my hero* (Circaidy Gregory Press 2015)

Rose Flint 'Prayer for Always Peace' and 'Running on Empty' are from *Mother of Pearl* (PS Avalon)

Margie Gaffron 'Cabin Fever' first appeared in *Holdings* by the author, a Fell/Design Book

Caroline Gill 'Weddell Seal at the Ice Edge' was initially published in *Visible Breath* (Indigo Dreams Publishing, 2010)

Jan Harris 'Surprising Times' was published in *Nth Position* April 09 and *Caught in the Net* (Poetry Kit Series) April 2012.

Marc Harshman 'Mousehole' and 'What There Is' are from *Green-Silver and Silent* (Bottom Dog Press)

Mark Haworth-Booth 'Water Sonnet' was first published in *South*

Tania Hershman 'Hold The Baby' was first published in *Butcher's Dog Issue 2*. 'The Weight Of Us' was first published in the *Canterbury Poet of the Year Anthology 2014*

Siham Karami 'Letter to Asma Al-Assa' previously published in *New Verse News*

Wendy Klein 'The Word for Lost in Swahili'was commended in the Ver Poetry Competition (2014) and published in the competition anthology. 'Morning News 'was published in *Artemis*

Desmond Kon Zhicheng-Mingdé 'After Emphysema' previously published in *Hour of Writes*

Camilla Lambert 'Curly Leaves all Dance as the Wind Blows' will be published in the author's poetry pamphlet from Indigo Dreams Press 2015

Alison Lock 'Kandahar' was published in the poetry collection *A Slither of Air* (Indigo Dreams Publishing, 2011)

Rupert Loydell 'Ordinary' was first published in *Tears in the Fence*

Lennart Lundh 'Plus Tarde, Les Langues Des Amateurs' was published in the author's *Poems Against Cancer*

Paul Matthews 'A Gratitude' was previously published in *Slippery Characters* (Five Seasons Press)

John Mc Mcullough 'Sleeping Hermaphrodite' and 'Talacre' were first published in *The Frost Fairs* (Salt 2011)

Gill McEvoy 'There's a Grey Parrot, 'Magpie' 'The Cuckoo' were first published in *The First Telling* (Happenstance 2015)

Helen Moore 'Monsoon June' was published in *Hedge Fund, And Other Living Margins* (Shearsman Books, 2012)

Mary E.Moore 'Last Communion' was published in *The Mid-America Poetry Review*

Irena Pasvinter 'I am a Ship' was first published in *Every Day Poets*

Jay Ramsay 'Hot Tub' was previously published in *Neo-Nature* (Chrysalis Poetry, 2013)

Susan Richardson 'Nereid' was published in *skindancing* (Cinnamon Press 2015)

Robert Schechter 'I look for life in death' first published in *Leviathan Quarterly*

Gordon Simms 'Estuary' appeared in *New Writer* 2010

Jocelyn Simms 'Market Day' was published by Earlyworks Press

Richard Skinner Four poems from the author's collection, *the light user scheme* (Smokestack 2013),

Susan Skinner 'The Wind is in the Rose' was first published in *Out of Nowhere* (Searle Publishing)

Wendy Sloan 'Dead Young Thing' originally published in *The Raintown Review*

Beth Somerford 'Putting the Garden to Bed' was first published in *Messing with Endings* 'Different'

Anne Stewart 'The Spanish Islands' was included by the Poetry Society in their *Lucky Dip: Take a Poem Home* project in 2010.

Seán Street 'On Not Being There' was first published in *Cello* (Rockingham Press 2013)

Susan Taylor 'Theatre of Now' was first published in *The Suspension of the Moon* (Oversteps Books 2006)

Eilidh Thomas 'Malala Dreams' was published in *The Stares Nest* July 2014

Jackie Wills 'Day of Rest' and 'Letter' are from *Commandments* (Arc)

Shirley Wright 'Arête' won the 'People's Prize' at the Wells International Literature Festival, 2014

Poems for a Liminal Age
is dedicated to the bold and selfless spirits
of the medical professionals in Médecins Sans Frontières
who would go to the very end of the earth itself,
sometimes at great personal risks,
to fight for the life of every member of
the human family.

Contents

Preface

At the start of this project I was invited to choose the theme of the anthology and the charity we hoped would benefit. I think I am speaking for everyone involved in this publication when I say how pleased and proud I am that part of the proceeds from sales of the book will be going to support Médecins Sans Frontières in its generous and courageous efforts to relieve and prevent suffering across the world. I was particularly attracted to the international and independent nature of this rganization with its credo that the needs of people outweigh considerations of national borders and that everyone has the right to humanitarian care, regardless of race, religion, creed or political affiliation.

It is an extra joy to me that making a donation has not just been a matter of writing a cheque or handing over cash, but has involved expressions of care and small acts of creation through the medium of words.

'Liminal' is an ambiguous term with several shades of meaning, lending itself to many subtle interpretations, as shown in this book. For myself, I suppose I see it as a word suggesting thresholds, transition, a midpoint, a space between possibilities, but throughout the editing process I have been concerned to let contributors select their own spiritual, social, political, cultural or philosophical approaches to the theme.

No doubt people who lived in other centuries considered their own ages to be liminal – uncertain, on the edge and frightening. My feeling is that this present age may come to be seen as particularly so. It is a time of rapid and intense change with a huge potential for tragedy and disaster but also, one hopes, for enlightenment.

Poems for a Liminal Age offers a view of the way a certain group of people at a certain time in their planet's history see their lives and the world they live in. The poems, taken together, make for fascinating if not comfortable reading. Many present an impression of bleakness in situations of confusion, loneliness, sickness, mediocrity and boredom. There is a sense of waste, of goodness being squandered, of corruption, brutality and loss. Other poems, however, evoke a sense of becoming, a feeling for nostalgia, beauty, trust and friendship, an impression of longing and the possibility of vision.

Loads of thanks to all the poets who have contributed their fine pieces to this anthology, to the many people across the globe who are supporting this project with enthusiasm, and particularly to Nnorom Azuonye of SPM Publications who had the brilliant idea of an anthology in the first place and has brought the concept to fruition.

I am very grateful to have had the pleasure of editing *Poems for a Liminal Age* and I wish the book, the poets and especially MSF all the luck in the world.

Mandy Pannett

Poems for a Liminal Age

Mary E. Moore

LAST COMMUNION

At first light,
on the deserted inlet shore,
a long-tailed duck, fallen on its side –
only its head thrusts upwards –
struggles to stand.
Again and again it fails.

A woman approaches,
backs off, walks away.

She returns burdened,
kneels beside the bird,
pillows its head
with one of two large stones.
With a fingertip, she strokes a wing.
She lifts the other stone high,
strikes.

Wendy Klein

MORNING NEWS

My half-blind Spaniel blunders into a table leg,
just hard enough to upset my coffee,

and off to the kitchen for a cloth, I'm stopped
by the clipped voice of the Today Programme,

flood reports – am riveted by an item about a couple
pushing a pram beside a rising river, dogs

at their heels, skittish on an afternoon out, and I find myself
with them in the rowdy wind, feel the first drops of rain;

watch the water, high and wide-bellied, as one dog leaps
to fetch a ball tossed midstream in play,

see how he's followed into the torrent by the second,
a Springer or a Lab, how in a moment's breath,

the mother realises the mistake, screams *my God, they'll drown,*
wades in, stumbles as their heads bob, disappear,

bob again; how the father dives to rescue the family pets,
his wife; leaves the pram, the sleeping child,

the commentator says, *without* setting the brake;
how the surge consumes them with silent greed,

rushes on, bloated and indifferent, the baby wailing,
the pram floating at first; how the cloth in my hand,

un-squeezed, floods the floor, soaks my slippers, leaves
me aghast, starting to wonder what I might have done.

Jim Bennett

TIMES SQUARE AT MIDNIGHT

in New York I stay just off Times Square
so I can walk round and stand at midnight
wide eyed amongst the wide eyed
watch as cops and yellow cabs pose
pretend not to take pictures   while
I take pictures   stay there until three
in the morning   it is like it always is
like I imagined it was going to be
I am a fish in a pond unable see stars
but everywhere light catches on scales
trapped in colours that shine and change
impossible to see detail in the reflections
that flash on every surface   here I am now
a butterfly or moth I never know which

Rupert Loydell

ORDINARY

I live in a world where epiphanies
are for sale everywhere, and magic
is an everyday occurrence. Wonder
carries me through the nights,
helps me improvise take offs
and landings wherever I am
called to go. Across the water
trains became your death
and there is no trace of the plane
that disappeared last week.

Possibly, we turned back
on ourselves and headed elsewhere;
whatever the conclusion it remains
a mystery and concern. I am in
a strange place where the sun
never seems to shine and people
around me keep dying. The boat
is broken again and I am losing
the will to make repairs or sail it
around the edges of long days

at work or the few weekends
we salvage from rehearsals
and clubs. I am rarely alone
and when I am I wish I wasn't;
New York mornings were never
like this. Down by the river,
birds sing whether it rains or not
and the colour of fields is always
changing; by the time I have mixed
my paint the light flickers or dulls,

clouds crawl across the water,
shadowing the page. If we drive up early
we will have enough time for a drink,
if we drink the night before we will
not get up in time to give our talk.
Buses go from the hotel to there,
are probably the simplest way
to cross the city. Everything
feels like a major exercise,
there are always too many things

to do. The washing is out to dry,
the fridge restocked with food;
entries for the village show
must be in before tomorrow.
The sleeping constellations
slowly move below the horizon,
night comes and goes in our dreams.
Epiphanies happen without me,
blessings lope into the beyond.
My world is such an ordinary place.

Matthew Wilson

DIANA DIES

We have no light but glint of uninterested stars
We power batteries by wind and work and water
Squinting in our candlelight or writing poetry
Promise of hope, fairytales for son and daughter.

These are black border now, these cold peaks of night
When winged things, thankfully unseen sweep past
Watching at windows with their yellow winking eyes
When we hope our weak defenses hold till morning fast.

We have to make our own light sources now
To keep away the bogeyman they said
Warnings of monsters that parents preach
To drag naughty children beneath their bed.

We have such little time to enjoy the sun now
Smarter men than I have spoken of this doom
When the womb of Helios sinks behind the borders
Now that damned dragons eaten the moon.

Marc Woodward

ACCORDING TO A RECENT POLL OF RELIGIOUS BELIEFS ...

I don't believe in *Gallup.*
Or that there's a *Mori.*

The theory that all life began
following a great brain-storm
and product placement plan:
"The Big Water Cooler Moment"
- and we all evolved, winding
through an endless torrent
of market research findings
and feedback analysis tools,
should never be taught in schools.

For science has proven
that long before advertising,
there was life.
True, it didn't always
know what it wanted
or how to look good,
how to have *"allure"*,
but it was there.
Prehysterical and pure.

Eilidh Thomas

TIME TO PAINT THE HEATHER

I know you don't want to be here
when the call comes
and you've drawn
the short straw

But like it or not
you're on the list...
without your consent

It's not about bravery
or cowardice
there's no apologies
or forgiveness

So enjoy the summer
go for a walk
take time
to paint the heather
in case it doesn't bloom
again for you

Watch waves roll
and dolphins jump
near to shore

Play at skipping ropes
until you can skip no more

Miles Salter

YOU ARE STANDING ON A PLATFORM

You are standing on a platform.
The train has not arrived.

You watched the others leave
on different trains, days ago,

with their children and small cases,
then tried to sleep in the waiting room.

It will not be long now, the Station Master says.
You think of home. Your brother, for instance:

was there a moustache? A medal?
A leaf rattles along the track.

Soon you will depart. Fifty miles east,
a man inspects a list that contains your name.

S. M. Beckett

WINTER IN CARONI

Amethyst clouds push darkness
over the hills where a man walks his life
through umber shadows. Nothing shines

except three plastic flowers - yellow flares
stuck in the ground by a roadside grave –
sweeter than any stone angel.

The sky drowns in a pond
white egrets stand quiet as a sigh.

II

In the bar men slump over tables
sitar music sobbing into their rum.
The gas station closed, weeds straggle

across tarmac. At the roadside parlour
there is little to buy – a few dasheen
some wilted baji, an onion or two.

The village is forgotten
there is no work.

III

The man walks on head bowed
through the heave and sough
of uncut cane, past the silent

Sugar Plant, making his way,
step by step round old landmarks,
over the rise and fall of memory.

The land is orphaned
the Mango trees are mute.

Afam Akeh

SELECTIONS FROM 'ENDNOTES'

My little boy
asking little boy questions

believes by asking
he can know all about it.

As I once did

alone with you, asking
about rivers and mountains,

people and planets …

I see you lying down,
your babies and their babies

leaning over, the joy
of drum outside.

Drums are joyful
whatever the weather -

as flutes are not.

It is you and not I, as
shorn sheep or plucked bird,

as there and not there,

What is most present
is absence – vacant face,

faded colour, the shrinking
of that forehead

so dominant
in your fortieth photo.

Under the awnings
the wine is every moment.

Folk talk and sing.
You are their tale retold.

*

I listen to reclaim
your voice

and hear only echoes.

Flashes
of stories left behind.

Loss is so silent.

It rises early
with a busy schedule

of things to end,
loves and lives,

new hearts to break,

the rage of the world
at his heels.

Returns in silence

after dark

to share my bed, still
full of files, and

will not speak, will not
answer my questions.

*

You had a thing about alien beds,
hospitals, hotels, alien soil.

You had thought it out
as you did all things,

planning for all seasons.

Your own bed in your own house,
breathing the familiar odours.

And properly finished,

All farewells said, your earth
to earth in familiar humus.

Stomping dirt
in a foreign land, I

inherit the wind
and the comfort of strangers.

What are these ties that bind?

Sometimes you choose your earth,
sometimes your earth chooses you.

Tania Hershman

HOLD THE BABY

They said she had to hold the baby so she held the baby even
though she had no notion why she held it, him or her. They said
she couldn't look to see so in her mind she thought of it as both,
a Jenny and a James, and she knew it wasn't right but there was
nothing more to say. They said they'd run some tests while she
was holding it, experiments of a sort, but she was not so clear
on what sort. Perhaps they measured angles, how she held it,
how it sat there. Maybe they counted breaths, hers or its, or
maybe blood flow or pressure, with machines she couldn't see.
Maybe they wired up her brain and knew what she was
thinking, feeling. Some time had passed, maybe minutes, and
then she wanted to drop the baby. Not hard, not on the floor,
just to not hold it any more.

Frances Gapper

SEAGULL

After my sister lost her house in the divorce she moved to live
with me, bringing with her a change of clothes and a book of
Anglo-Saxon poetry. When not asleep on the sofa she read The
Wanderer or The Seafarer (he chooses the harsh life of the sea
over a land of dead pleasures where there are no givers of gold)
and watched seagulls floating over the rooftops. At least they're
free, she sighed. So I wasn't surprised when one day I came
home from work to find she'd gone. A gull swooping past gave
one heart-piercing farewell cry.

MOURNING ANGEL

The mourning angel we installed on our mother's grave is like a
crying doll, only 6ft high. Tears are piped through holes in her
bronze eyes, from a storage tank fixed under her wings at the
back. This tank didn't have much capacity, so my brother ran a T
off the pipe to the cemetery tap, adding a solar-powered pump.
Now on sunny days instead of dribbling down her face the tears
shoot upwards and fall in a sparkling shower on the gravel path.

CATCHING FIRE

The smallest things made him angry. He would light a fire in the
cranky old woodburning stove and instruct her to keep it alive.
But however hard she tried, the fire always went out, suffocated
by its own smoke. Glancing through the window, she noticed a
clump of snowdrops under the sycamore. Every year they took
her by surprise. A fluttering distracted her, was it in the garden
or the field, or – she pressed a hand above her belly, felt it,
invisible but here. Would she tell him? No, she decided. And
knew she must leave this place.

STEPMOTHER

Although he didn't exactly choose me, I was a good
housekeeper, found adequate to fill his ex-wife's position. Make
do and mend. But the kids flew and clung to me, like nails to a
magnet. Poor ugly little rejects; I found pity to be no weak
emotion. Then I gave birth to my own child, he suckled at my
breast. The scrawny kids hung around our Madonna-and-son
tableau. I must love this baby, I told myself. But love didn't come
naturally.

Alwyn Marriage

MOVING ON

The first time I heard you speak of *home*,
not meaning the house where I live
and where you'd spent your childhood,
there was a slight, but perceptible
shuddering in my foundations.

Flesh from my flesh, ever since your journey
started I had been letting go;
but feared this visible and physical
realignment to our world
might lead to the final separation.

Time proved the opposite; but for a while
I had to watch while you learnt to adjust
to life in a place you didn't know, while I,
just as tentatively, grew accustomed
to a home empty of you.

Jay Ramsay

SACRIFICIAL STONE
Rennes-le-Chateau

Shadow under the mountain, exhumed
a single block of blond stone the length of a bed
for the head to be forced, the feet to be stretched
bound, terrified in surrender: the crude bowl
for a heart's blood scooped out
clawed, chanted out ... filled with tan rainwater now
even in the heat of the day, and pocked
with fragments of rubbish. Two crosses
incised at its edge, like an exorcism ...
Abraham and Isaac making their way
as you trail your child's wrist with its bright
loom bands, as we gaze down: the same sky above
with its imagined God no greater than our minds
the God of Sacrifice, or the God of Love.

David Caddy

FOR A WEEK IN MAY 1968

Water dazzled, dozens of effects
lure daily marks of level and passage.
The scene always beyond capture,
perspective held by what remains.

Chub were visible late afternoon.
Early crabapples appeared in profusion.
The cart horse was mysteriously led away
amid cries of malo-lactic fermentation.

The return was lapse, a thrill,
orders blipped and slapped the face
of the river, tetchy with low usage
and Mill tenant burps.

Onion men sat on their bicycles
schoolboys wrestled in bed with transistors,
gypsies took their pegs and luck to town,
the milling conveyed to famish and dwindle.

Butter would not come, barren cows sold,
venture payout delayed, certainties slip,
sluice gates well oiled and unmoved,
eels thick in mud beneath watermark.

Paul Matthews

SPEAKING FOR HERMES

Was I a god way back?
I can't remember.

Here now is the ground
where you might know me.

Admittedly it's a thin place
easily passed over.

Furnish it with an altar
if you need one, then

sit quietly until winged
sandals lift you.

A thief is what I am,
that's true, yet I squander

silver at the crossroads
for quick eyes to catch.

I pun, and play the liar.
Oh, but I turn sad

when a bluebell stared at
loses lustre.

Meet me in the crossfire
between the words I write.

Aprilia Zank

THE DEATH OF THE FISHER KING
to Robin Williams

he dug out his fire stallion...
from under the ambers of the altar
put on his barbed wire crown

followed the traces of blood
of rats nagging at drowsy derelicts
in underground corridors

of lovers castigated by sniper gods
for having chosen the wrong place
in the wrong moment

of ghost cast shadows
tumbling in the squeeze of his skull
as he dragged his golden rags in the tunnels –

and how long can a man walk on water
to get a glimpse of the Grail
shimmering in the depths of the well?

not farther than a dream's length
not farther than the vault of a second
not farther than an owl's call in the dead of night

and how long can a man
walk into and out of a dream
without tattering its ephemeral carcass?

how long can a man
wipe off the blood on his hands
of deeds he has never begotten?

he put on his crown of burning feathers
mounted his stallion armoured with flames
vanished into the well following the call of the Grail

Penny Hope

INSTRUCTIONS FOR THE MASK WEARER

Let not your lips betray you.
Purse and pucker, smile askew.
Suck the lips inwards
for the thinning,
Colour beyond the natural line
for the thickening.

Where the mouth is concealed,
make much of muffled speaking.

Let not your speech betray you.

Know your own voice
that you may lose it.
Sing discordantly
where harmony is your wont.

Do not to betray yourself in the moving,
Learn your own gait
that you may lose it.
Make yourself tall, adopt the stoop,
but better shun the limp than limp lamely.

He who has most success
is most natural in the feigning.

Let not your hands betray you.
Many have fallen foul of the finger freckle.

Wear gloves, mantle and such adornments
of the head and neck as are befitting.

Remember the wayward plume
begets the untamed chuckle.
Besmear yourself with thyme,
honeysuckle, garlic,
and other pungencies
lest you be unraveled
by your own odours.

Make merry, though you be not merry,
for many are made merry in the making.

Cavort with the best jesters in the city.

Clench the mask surely to the visage.
Suffer all manner of chafings,
aches and irritations of arm and jaw.
He who endures
will be rewarded.

Listen to your inward purpose
as you pretend yourself outwardly.

Be unobserved in your observing.
Breathe only through the eyes.

Martin Elster

THE LONELIEST ROAD

Another planet grows and shrinks away,   the heliosphere an
ebbing memory,   you streaking like a wayward gamma
ray.   Around your vessel blooms a potpourri   of comet, nebula,
dark energy rushing you through the void, accelerating,   all you've
ever cared for quickly fading.

What road is lonelier than the universe?   For decades one could
sail and never stumble   across another soul. Things could be
worse.   Distracted, you could accidentally bumble   too close to a
cosmic gullet and wildly tumble,   yet really no more lost than
where you coast   past eagle, spider, witch-head, horsehead, ghost.

Though wandering through space entails great risk,   you have no
choice — the sun's begun to swell.   While moving at velocities as
brisk   as jets of interstellar wind, you smell   the rabbitbrush, the
desert breezes, dwell   on sounds of soughing yucca palms and
creeks,   glimpse bighorn bounding boulders, rusty streaks

of sunsets. As you near the edge of space,   you think of the stone
tools your forebears used   while breathing mayfly lives, a vanished
race   in tune with wilderness; and, though you've cruised   for
torrents of time now down this road suffused   with radiation, your
single mutant eye   still sees, not stars, but fireflies in July.

Note: The title alludes to Highway 50, The Loneliest Road in America.

48

Strider Marcus Jones

FADING SPHINX

another beautiful eye
reflects life's lie,
when you look into its face
and see a better place
close by.

without that circle round its dream,
everything is seen
to separate unequally in two
and drift apart blown through
old sky.

the why, where and when
does not matter then,
as it dissipates
into other fates
making old orders die.

in all the residue
of what we knew,
a fading sphinx, casting contemporary
shadows, rises, temporary
but still drops by

elsewhere, in the flawed foundations
of younger civilizations,
building their own
mountains of shaped stone
where polished lenses spy.

Michael Cantor

THE JOURNALIST

The *when* came first, and was no problem since
clocks hung on the market wall had stopped
precisely at the time he had to know,
and there were watches too, all smashed it seemed,
and parts of straps, and down the blackened street
a grand old tower timepiece still retained
an hour hand; and what was good was that
they all agreed: there was no fog or mystery.

Where was simple also, since the maps
and GPS coordinates all showed *this village*
or *that town*, and most had names, or he could
find someone to tell him *this is The-Street-
of-Music-Stores-That-Used-To-Be* or *here is
The Place-of-Orange-Trees-That-Burned-All-Night.*
He would write it down slowly, in his way,
and soon began to find the names himself.

He often stumbled, though, at *what*, for *what*
was not so clear. *Some kind of IED,*
they'd say, perhaps behind a truck or car.
Men came with masks and guns and called out names.
The belt is wrapped around a piece of corpse.
A woman, all in black, in line for food.
He learned more acronyms, and all the vast
new nuances that came with *improvised.*

And next was *who*, and *who* turned out to be
impossible. The bloodstains on stone walls
were *who*, and headless bodies found in lakes,
and gunners torched inside their vehicles,
and chunks of flesh and fat; and still the questions
rang of *who was this and who did that*,
and *who* was shot or bombed beyond all moral
sense, and *who* was God to suffer this?

And when he came to *why* he took a walk
at noon, behind a berm of blasted earth,
and stripped off forty pounds of Kevlar vest
and shirtless, spinning, spinning in the sun,
leaned against a rock, and puked, and wept;
but still the sun remained, and still he went
on going out each day to sanctify
the old, old cry: *who, what, when, where, why?*

Judith Cair

THE LOCK AT FLATFORD

The Stour was flowing fast towards the lock; ahead of us
an old black dog, a Labrador, ambled along the path,
then walked in a diagonal (it must have been almost blind)
and fell into the water. We urged it to swim up to the side
but on it paddled, as the banks grew steeper and steeper,
the surface of the water further from reach.

It came to the lock; weaker now, it began to flail,
turning in tiny circles, head up, body heavier and heavier.
The only way down to it was by a ladder attached to the wall –
a vertical descent to the black water and the weight
of a helpless animal to come. We gazed at the dog
who circled feebly anticlockwise lower and lower
in the water, with just its muzzle showing, and a gasp.

Not an inch could I move towards the ladder. To know myself
a coward as the dog whimpered. I ran to the mill,
to ask for a free-standing ladder (though how would it
take root in that dark water?) The woman raged at us,
"What kind of people stand by and watch a dog drown?"
Fearless, she lowered herself down the struts, hauled
the old dog up. It lay on the path exhausted, too much
water in its lungs for it to survive.

It was an old dog, almost blind; its owners should never
have let it stray by deep water. But for whose sake
would my limbs have taken me down that ladder?
To know myself a coward - to dread seeing Constable's
idylls and that dark lock where a dog or a woman could drown.

James Bell

A TASTE OF COFFEE

take a coffee at last
court avec sucre
and find it palatable after all

the vending machine remains inscrutable
nothing else in the world changes
though people who present
the news on TV are pink today

sip more coffee and realise
after all these years why the table
is called a coffee table

finish the coffee and feel
a brightening behind the eyes
a settling of the stomach

a long hum from the machine seems to suggest
I should have had a coffee before
and promise to take another tomorrow

see this as a development
it's like an easing of international tensions
where mutual intentions become clear

like most people who walk by
I might dress all in white -
something about angels comes to mind
but that's only caffeine and
           figments of the imagination

Patricia Ace

REFUGE

'Police say at least 30 people are sleeping permanently in Madrid airport's terminal 4' The Guardian , 2 January 2014

Luis has taken sanctuary at the airport.
In Terminal 4 he loses himself in thronging crowds
jostling trolleys across acres of high-gloss flooring,
luggage tagged with details of fixed abodes.

The passengers twitch and fidget, kept unsettled
by tic-like checking of watches, of phones.
Those delayed slump graceless on moulded seats
or splurge their Euros in the aisles of Duty Free.

Luis follows their contrails of sweat and perfume,
alcohol, coffee-breath, stale smoke and Clinique.
Sometimes they pay him to watch over their bags.
But when they move on, Luis goes nowhere,

stalled in this liminal portal, a twig in an eddy.
Each night he makes his bed, curled in a corner
on the cold marble tiles, his bones having their say.
At dawn he performs his washroom ablutions:

blessing the black sensor with a pass of his palm,
he washes his hair in the font of the sink, stoops,
dripping and suppliant under the hand-drier.
Sometimes he stands by the rail at Arrivals,

wonders where his wife and kids are now. And
sometimes he stands before a wall of windows
watching the weather, the mackerel skies, the air
above the asphalt concertina'd by heat.

Jim Bennett

THE FLAT EARTH

today I could see why people thought
the world was flat   it looks flat   feels flat
as far as I can see it's flat   but it isn't
I can see its shadow across a daytime moon
the gentle curve of land through Arctic
Africa   Antarctica   folding into night

sometimes there is a line between
knowing and believing something
a train station gap that can trip you
when you least expect it   even when evidence
is clear   you don't want to see it
even things she said are hard to believe

until I remind myself about what I know
and that the world is round and the sound
on the beach   is the moon and dying ice
and land folds into mountains
how it came to be   how it moves
how the movement of time changes everything

Oonah Joslin

TO THE JOURNEY

The girl on the train sips at her drink; gazes with longing
through the beaded rain travelling beside her across pane and
plane, streaking distant white topped hills in veins blue-grey;
imagining alternate destinations.

TORONTO GIRL

slender quick how you think no consonants no consequence no
breaks events through the day like cup of coffee double shot no
lid no lip you flit among high rise traffic fumes and sun-glint
twenty four carat bank finger-sampling sushi mall-bites a
fluttering cyber-walk mannequin ear-plugging louder to drown
the surround sound long into the slim-line stream-line uniform
casino Niagara night falls

restful dawn
golden girl awakes
another gadget-day to go

HAIKU

Far away cultures
meet on peaceful horizons.
On beaches they clash.

John Freeman

IT WAS US

Something led me to mention the time
twenty years before when we had stayed
in a cottage on the Isle of Wight,
our brief apogee, and she laughed
softly, sadly, deprecatingly.
I insisted, that was us, *c'était nous*.
She stopped laughing and accepted
the point I was making, whatever it was –
perhaps that our lives had been as real
as her having to let go of life was,
and that the understanding between us
now could connect with the harmony
then, the nearest we ever came.
I'd swum and talked, she'd danced and sung,
we'd walked by the sea and under trees.
Outside there had been cold rain and wind,
bracing. Inside was an open fire, stillness,
a vase of honesty and tall grass
on the mantelpiece that became
an emblem of that time, our time.
C'était nous. That settled, we got on,
me helping her as well as I could
with what she had to go through alone,
but able to accept my company
and loyalty right up to the tree-line
or the snow-line, and even beyond,
where the love welcoming her was
more than my own, I could feel it
shaping my face to smile at her, see it
in the way she smiled at something through me.

Richard J.N. Copeland

THE WATCHERS

They drift by, soft shoe silent,
checking in for the morning shift.
A moment's recognition holds them
as attention focuses its instant
with a greeting, a glance and a smile
before work begins with notes,

observations read and comments added:
the meds, the sats, the drugs,
all these and so much more
while time ticks by unseen
in a place that has no time
and a minute is all that lies

between a whispered word and zero,
a touch of sightline to connect
the singularity of being one to another
to make this entity
that in its eyelid flicker chimes
the notes that sound elsewhere.

At times they gather to share small talk,
happy to relax with news and laughter,
stories from the pub or home, still never
far from the eyes that stare mutely
beseeching only air to watch
till one of them returns.

Peter Branson

GHOSTS

Back bedroom and the parlour underneath,
fireplace of rough-sawn stone and polished slate,
the part that used to be his cramped farmstead,
is where all this takes place. Wood-burning stove
is never lit, so there's no tendency
to linger there; year-long you feel the chill.
The kitchen is the space she likes to dwell,
framed by the hearthside's gilding under-glow.
Next door he taps his pipe against the grate,
refills, strikes up. She smells tobacco, hears
his old man's cough-and-hack into the grate,
the chatter of hobnail on flag, discerns
his little dog scrape by into the hall.
Each morning she puts food out for the birds,
nest-boxes everywhere, garden and wood.
She leaves her husband once: "Plenty of time,"
yet when they try, no luck! The only one
she carries through to term is damaged goods,
conceives her canker as a punishment.
Some nights, the cradle ticking like a faint
heartbeat, a live time bomb inside her head,
she hears the cello. Locals tell he played
slow airs when beasts came near their time or yields
were low. The place was blessed with life; kids thrived,
pitched in amongst the calves and lambs, way back.
Half dressed, she conjures him, deep voice, in welsh,
severe. Strong arms wrap round her waist; rough hands
expose her belly, breasts, between her thighs,
as though examining a troubled ewe.
"What are you doing here? Why have you come?"

Seán Street

ON NOT BEING THERE

1

An idea on the edge of an image
preserved intact, thought described to itself
across distance and existing over
horizon's lake of possibility
just beyond the prose of the physical,
its essence an aura light, unbroken
by the crude iron rust fact of matter,
real, but coolly outside the literal.

11

A reflection risked against Time,
it's all there as you recall it,
a straight road arcing up to woods
in a child's sky. Place has a right
to change, but now look, you retain
ownership through the same autumn
branches a fractured photograph
recovered on behalf of your past.
Nothing remembered ever dies.
What of this slight light evening rain?
There's still enough of a sunset
to turn these trees to silhouettes,
told to yourself through memory,
a reality repossessed.

111

A fraction of amber, a silver thread,
seeds and a coin and some thin green glass.
Tiny things in so much, so much earth,
called back to air from their distant light
under crowding centuries. As storms shout
at the bay past the headland's frail bulwark,
they search for long-lost whispers through strata.
The slow soil clock rewinds, human kin lie
waiting, gasping somewhere in all this silt.
The sea's same sound issues across first places.
Crouched on these cold islands they sieve for gifts,
mortality's forgotten things to clasp hands,
understandings to bridge at last living
and dead, their mutuality a shared place,
facilitating encounter as time
runs out just above the tide line. They search
here on behalf of us to show who we
might have been. Guided by cartography
from a fallible rumoured tradition
and inadequate documentation,
they are digging desperately for some clue,
delve and scrape, seeking something - be it thread,
a bead, a seed - just anything to salve
this exclusion, loneliness. Anything.

IV
(*Incandesce:* Acrylic on Canvas, Jemma Street)

A window opaque but open
onto a world. A sky drawn down,
paint's catch gathered to a canvas,
caught alive, brought into a room
to remain there in place and time
as changing light accumulates.

A doorway for light opening
to a space without walls or floor.
Not being there I can't explain
past your given premonition,
windows and doors that will open
from unbuilt halls into air,
gathering today for new time,
speaking for us, not being there.

Rachael Clyne

DODGY LEADS

Here is the atrium, ventricle and mitral valve
a septum to divide the giving from receiving side
mark how each systole, diastole pumps the flow
how aorta spouts to root and branch, a scarlet tide
to all extremities a body can provide
mark the gentle flow of crimson cells for fresh supply.

Mesmerised by the green line that traces its course
of never-ending rhythm in alpine troughs and peaks
the lup-dup of my life, while nervously I seek
for some minute anomaly that suggests a fatal flaw
learn to pronounce such terms as 'dodgy lead'
and troponin, then wonder what they mean.

On the trolley in A&E, I sing *'Happy Birthday'* to me
strapped to my arbiter of fate, until results return
gaze at this intimate detail of my existence
the moment by moment beauty of its gift
how it transports chemicals of wonder, love, or hate
how it starts and ends in a heartbeat.

Anna Crowe

THE HINTERLAND

This is a world turned inside-out,
a republic of the flesh
both strange and strangely familiar.

The walls are hung with oils,
portraits of common soldiers
who fought at Corunna or Waterloo,
where Charles Bell, army-surgeon,
paints the sun going down in musket-wounds,
with full colours, in a glory that pale flesh
puts on before nightfall.

Tables are ceremoniously laid
with dishes of sprigged china, glassware,
entire canteens of polished cutlery:
here are tools for cutting and slicing,
for gripping and probing; even a saw.
But though the cabinets are replete
with choice cuts, the guests
left years ago, when their bodies grew
to homes they couldn't call their own.

As though flesh were determined to cross
a threshhold into metaphor, blossoming,
hardening into vegetable or mineral forms
both beautiful and deadly –
unnatural fruit sprouting from floorboards,
timbers shivering into Flemish lace;
one with Crohn's Disease departing
when her bowel became a draper's shop,
stuffed to the gills with pleated satin;

others retreating as from a volcano
when X-rayed lungs threw up
carcinomas bright as agates, when skin
erupted in melanomas black as basalt.

Inner forms call up the presences of plants:
our nervous system, fine as asparagus-fern,
is sheathed like fennel; our arteries branch
like rosy nets of *corallina* left by the tide –
morphologies of flow, like the child's plait
the Amazon makes, seen from the moon.
Who can doubt that water was once our home,
seeing these skeletons of foetal hands?
Poised in jars of formalin,
these minute brown transparent bones,
are articulated like marine crustacea,
delicate as the bodies of shrimps.
They are travellers from the hinterland
whose journey ended before it began,
fish-bones, writing their brief histories
in runes, in ogham-script the colour of blood;
whose perfect, counted fingers
make my eyes swim with salt.

Pansy Maurer-Alvarez

WE FIT IN A ROOM

We fit in a room, a quiet room, and in a minute, shiver
cradling the old question sadly diminished in stillness
This makes me curious and eager for meaning
Is this the natural feeling after all these years?

Not prepared to   does not mean
unprepared   from a distance resembling a smoke wreath
The Sirens have drowned the sound of rupture and the morning
offers its gathering of animated shapes against another light
A natural feeling starting to come apart, becomes basic
that we might have already come to the final room

And if I bring to the table what I have found
the error of what I have found
and put it all into words
not necessarily harsh but lengthy, distorted, would you be
concerned, or if not concerned, curious?

Your left eye, profile, ear, the sheen on your skin from
          my angle beside you
We've come to our table now unable to speak
for fear of becoming unreal and separated
A gray memory of waiting in a Belgian lobby
watching passersby through a vine-darkened window
They could be anyone going anywhere
Everyone here is going someplace
I thought then not knowing

We live among our things, pressed next to people
knowledgeable with questions
and this is the way some stories are told —
to imagine ourselves, others   what facts there are
"This is our jubilation
Exalted and as old as that truthfulness
Which illumines speech."
A good cook   her cheek, her mouth and kitchen scales
beyond the rim of her plates   light-headed
distinctly dislocated, unruly yet sufficient
"It is not the wild glare
Of the world even that one dies in."
What was it, that single thing I wanted more than anything?

Quotations from "Of Being Numerous" by George Oppen

Marc Harshman

MOUSEHOLE

On that knotted and splintered
upturned boat of rock
white-washed with surf
Merlin stood and
what he said is
not so important,
though here, behind the breakwater,
these seventeenth century stone houses
remind me that Mousehole did,
in fact, burn to the ground,
and he didn't know, well, didn't say,
it would be Spaniards
 angry the Armada
was lost, and vengeful that a
Mousehole man had seen
a scudding Spanish cloud
whiter than mist
and so tipped off the English fleet.
Difficult to believe even now
the lengths to which we will go,
as they did, to return
to the zealotry of killing
for God and King,
difficult to believe
that one man could stand so *outside*,
could weather here the blow of a full gale,
have the patience to wait
the nights of storm for visions
and then have the clever nerve
to whisper them into the world.
How long would I practice
on this safe shore

in sight of that same, small
gull-and-tern-spotted spit of stone,
practice standing alone
and facing into the wind learn
to lash myself to the heart,
hear through the gale of silence?

Mousehole: *Mousehole, pronounced "mou-zul," is the name of the coastal village in Cornwall where this incident took place.*

Catherine Ayres

RETURN TO CONISTON WATER

If I chose to forget
I would sit by the lake
stretched like a lapse
in this memory of light.

If I chose to forget
I would skim its pale stone
let my arms drift like snow
fold their white into white.

If I chose to forget
I would swallow the grace
of the water's slate mouth
a sharp tooth in its bite.

Robert Schechter

I LOOK FOR LIFE IN DEATH

from the Spanish of Miguel de Cervantes

I look for life in death;
health, in infirmity;
in prison, liberty;
in suffocation, breath;
and faith in treachery.

But destiny (which I
have never prospered by)
has issued its decree.
"Demand what cannot be,
what can, I will deny."

The original Spanish:

Busco en la muerte la vida

Busco en la muerte la vida,
salud en la enfermedad,
en la prisión libertad,
en lo cerrado salida
y en el traidor lealtad.

Pero mi suerte, de quien
jamás espero algún bien,
con el cielo ha estatuido,
que, pues lo imposible pido,
lo posible aún no me den.

Roselle Angwin

LET US SPEAK OF THOSE THINGS TOO

It happens that the new moon is rising
hesitant and virginal over the serrations of slate
high above us above the Atlantic above where the dog-fox
the night before had crept by, its mouth grinning
round someone's pet white rabbit
                         as you are speaking of yet
another loss after these years of it
and I watch your face, its serenity, its severity –
the nun in you under the laughter. When
you'd asthma as a child you'd wheeze and then whistle
wheeze and whistle, something coin-bright in you
glittering still under clear water
                         not broken
by the past's long turbulence, by
the journey out of Africa – the marigold
of the present moment always trying to rise
to make a bloom of your face. The way
you don't say that you speak with angels
and demons.

                 Driving back in July dusk,
Wales stretching out an arm across the unrippled sea
hay-scent and elderflower thick enough
to hijack the car and my driving of it
into another country, erotic, secret, night-time
                      I'm jinked from freewheeling
by a memory of the woman thrown down the well,
the sniper in the trees, the voices
that turned you around in terror, disasters
you seem to know about before they happen
seeds of the past forescribing the future.

I pull over, unsure
what I'm wanting to stop for. I'm suspended
between sense and meaning, dusk and its questions
misting my hair. I suppose we're all doing nothing
but the best we can. I suppose we all
catch ourselves out, being unsure who we are
or what we might have come for.

Paul Matthews

A GRATITUDE
(*for Elizabeth Edmunds*)

Sit down, Elizabeth. This plastic chair
outside the Bridgeway Café in Sausalito
is empty especially for you,
and I have an hour to spare
before I catch the Ferry.

You died four days ago five thousand
miles from where I sit in the sun
expecting any moment
a rumbling under San Francisco Bay
to shake the froth on my Cappuccino.

It is a chair unfit, I confess,
to honour your ancient blood;
but before the currents carry you out
beyond the Golden Gate
I have a gratitude that must be spoken

for myself and anyone
who met you in the halls back home,
your sly smile, your gaze wide as ocean:
Thank you for speaking to the person
I could become.

Judith Cair

LOPPED

the great blue conifer –
fallen and its place

is empty. The rope
has been pulled tight

against lifted voices;
across the gardens nothing

lives behind my eyes.
Bird on the highest point,

outlined against the sky,
you are mind-bird now.

Vanessa Gebbie

ON BEING IN THE WRONG MOOD

to take seriously a suggestion from Bernard O'Donaghue to write a
poem at a workshop: 'On Not'

Who, or why, or which or what
is the pelagical, tragical Island of Notte?

Is it big or small, or wet or dry
Do the populace blunder and dawdle or fly? Or trot?
                        On the Island of Notte?

Do they catch their eagles in shrimping nets
and wait for spring before taking bets? On what?
                        On the Island of Notte.

While polishing pebbles and harpooning trees,
languages aplenty they speak with great ease. Polyglot,
                        the island of Notte.

Do they make a classic Irish stew
with lamb, potato and onion too? Or shallot?
                        On the Island of Notte?

Are they Left or Right or somewhere between?
Is she Welsh, American or Irish, their Queen? Or a Scot?
                        On the Island of Notte?

Does the king sail a boat at the end of each day,
then scupper them all in a most silly way? Clot.
                        On the Island of Notte.

In summer do icicles hang by the wall,
and no-one, no no-one goes swimming at all? Not hot,
                        the Island of Notte.

Do they treat misdemeanours in the strangest of ways
standing felons in treacle to the end of their days? Or garotte,
                            on the Island of Notte?

Are their poets poetical in ways parenthetical?
Do their novelists dither and dream? Or plot?
                    On the Island of Notte?

If they make a mistake whilst composing their words,
do they flap and tweet and pretend they are birds? Then they're
shot.
                        On the Island of Notte.

I was going to finish this poem most neatly.
Exactly how has escaped me completely. Forgot.
                        On the
incomprehensible, indispensible, utterly indefensible island
of Notte.

*With apols to Edward Lear, and to William Shakespeare Esq from
whome I nicked a line.*

Miles Salter

THE BUSKER

With buck teeth, banjo and a fuck it attitude,
he had an uncommon touch, belting out *Hard Travellin'*,
banjo strings clattering against apathy,

spitting words like a folk punk cowboy,
attitude snatched from The Clash and a tube of special
brew. A boozy scent clung to his neck.

Friday nights were best: chords ricocheting
off shuttered shops as packs of cheap lads
demanded *Wonderwall*, flinging

single quids at our feet. His flat was a tight,
dark space filled with tins and ashtrays.
'There's been some bother,' he said.
I looked around his tuneless cave, and nodded.

Gill McEvoy

THERE'S A GREY PARROT

chained to a perch at the back of the store.
Not my fault, not my fault, I tell him.

The bird cocks his head
and shuffles close
on gnarled grey claws.

Curtains his eyes in a blink.

MAGPIE

stabs itself under its wing
with that great beak.

Roots out vermin.

Hides the scar with feathers.

THE CUCKOO

has no conscience.
She roots out eggs from a nest.

Yolk stains the grass.

Jay Ramsay

MOTHER OF THE MORNING
for A.

Full summer – and while we were all loving it,
you'd seen the ground drying hard under the grass.
The blackbirds then, all pecking for worms on the lawn
and struggling: your big blue eyes missing nothing, ever.
'Especially after all those damn magpies', you said.

So you take the last apple and quarter it, 6 a.m,
then again. Six birds – you scatter the pieces,
broad as your heart, so they won't scrap over them;
then wait by the garden window to see them
before you come back to bed.

Those same eyes open beneath me now,
seeing all they can, in your countrywoman's mind,
as far divorced from narcissm as Israel from Gaza –
and the motherless daughter you are.

Martha Landman

OUR CORRUPTION

I was a child at play, stuck
in the sunflower fields of Africa
then a teenager in crimplene dress
on an upright chair in family portraits

ear stuck to the transistor radio,
I dreamt of the world of journalism
where stories have two sides or more
in the backroom, on vinyl floor

mother mopped and danced alone
to *Tulips from Amsterdam*
O how they feared for our corruption,
the Beatles, the Yellow Submarine.

Siham Karami

LETTER TO ASMA AL-ASSAD

As you were shopping for designer clothes,
My child was tortured by your husband's thugs,
The price to keep his job to buy you shoes.

Because we stood and chanted, "We refuse
This tyranny!" the bodies piled like jugs
While you were shopping for designer clothes.

He fights with tanks that no one can oppose.
From neighbors' rooftops snipers sink their slugs.
That's the price he pays to buy you shoes

That walk in the machinery of a ruse
To hide the human rubble as he shrugs,
So you can keep on shopping for the clothes

That lighten up his heart before he mows
Down men like grass, lets hospitals pull plugs --
The price to keep his job to buy you shoes

Whose path is getting rougher as it goes
Down darker where you can't tell men from bugs
And guts are dropping on designer clothes
And God knows where you're stepping with those shoes.

Bill Holdsworth

DREAMS AND REALITY

Walt Whitman dreamed a dream.
He saw a city invincible to the attacks of the whole wide world.
Walt Whitman dreamed of a city of friends.
I dream a dream. I see a city no longer drowning in its own
garbage.

In my good dream-times I see a city whose people's buses solar-
powered move on designated freeway tracks passing woods and
green pastures interleafing into places of comfortable habitation.

I dream again and find you Walt still hiding behind your full
grey-white beard asking Jane Jacobs if her sustainable cities will
stay alive.
And then to ask Wilhelm Reich and son Peter whether their
interpretations of sensual dreams are part of reality transplanted
from future time slips.

Instead I return to the conscious reality of an awakening day
where youngsters wander through pavement-lined burnt out
cars and conversation is no more.
A dream of black despair of a city parcelled into controlled zones
by convoys intersecting like prowler dogs.

Walt, Walt Whitman, did you see these dreams?
Walt, Walt Whitman, you with your aristocratic sense of spirit,
whose whole being was electric blue, who wanted man to
include the universe into his own being.
Will you have the drum taps played / the drum taps dressed in
pallbearers' velvet black.

It seems from my dream Walt that the world wants to die.

Aprilia Zank

MAN-MADE

she walks into the garden
stumbles across wall wreckage
searches
for the remains of some flowers
to hang above
the family photograph

so many missing now

not much left among the ashes
a few beheaded stalks
petals and stamina
scattered all over the place

she stoops down
digs with bare hands
under the ruins
for seeds
to plant in the spring

in the distance
growl and flashes
of man-made thunder
approach
relentlessly

Kyle Norwood

UNDER THE BLUE WIND

Welcome home: trees grown, pipes rusted, termites,
   rubble of excavation.

A stone house, a stream, sunken pond, lily pads,
   all gone now. I see them.

A harvest chill—red dresses after the dance—the
   library burns down.

House in flames: as we poured the foundation it
   was already burning.

Alexandria, Heraclitus is burning!
   Sappho is burning!

Thousand-year garden: intermittent flowers and
   ephemeral stones.

Horrified, Whitman praised the earth that eats corpses
   but is always clean.

The sage leaves light footprints, effaced by the breeze
   of his own passing.

Neil Howell

PHALIN

Cyclone Phailin punching west,
southpaw storm-surge hammering the coast
between Odisha and Andrha Pradesh.
Evacuate, escape, flee inland,
hurry, grab only what you cherish most,
scurrying children cling frantic to your hands.
Don't look back, leave doubt behind,
feel the fighter's sweat but don't let fear play the host.
It's shelter that you need, you seek, you find.
Hunker down behind closed doors,
brick-safe, food stock-piled, troops deployed in post
to save, sustain, protect you from the bully's roar.
Sit it out, bide your time, ride the storm,
cross-legged tell your stories, chatter, banter, brag, boast.
Share your lives, wait for calm to be re-born.
Return, distraught at the apocalyptic scene,
scour the flotsam, the scattered debris where you supposed
your hut, your house, your life, your home once had been.
Your tears dispel the anger, unfold the pain.
Phailin's energy is spent, dispersed, disposed
across the land where you must find the strength to start again.

James Bell

MAYBE THEY'LL MAKE THIS INTO A MUSEUM

after the next apocalypse
when there's not much left
and the coffee is good/better/worse
        than it is today -
when the vending machine still dispenses to tourists
who wander round in wonder
at this cultural artefact/primitive work of art
about to be closed off to the public
and a full size facsimile made to preserve
the original in perpetuity in
a controlled environment
so it is no longer damaged by tourists who
try to touch and breathe on various objects
        like the machine's buttons -
instead can stand in awe at
working models of apparatus
they say were once used to try and cure cancer
where it is difficult for them to imagine
how such ju-ju could have been effective
        with the disease -
and nobody will know what incantations
were used at what time and at what frequency
and what medicines were foraged
from fields and forests
and how it was known how to administer - will
only speculate on the side effects
when body parts were
exposed to doses
of radiation
to cure
rather than kill

Nnorom Azuonye

POSTCARDS FROM LONDON

1

At flight time, even choice had wings;
to stand still at life's gate in Kaduna,
until felled, perhaps by a Jihadist's sword,
to walk the world to night, feed the humour
of ex-friends maddened by defunct dreams,
or fly - fly away quickly to Great Britain...
but Great Britain is a merciless quicksand
that swallows decades of lives in a flash.

During honeymoon, the yet optimistic
hang around Trafalgar Square – carefree
idiots with double X wide smile syndrome
posing for photographs near Nelson's Column,
where pigeons fed-up with loveless tourists
dart past at hair level like war planes
and shoot movements from angry anuses
until the grinning lot become a bunch of shitheads.

2

Baby, this London sojourn has more twists in it
than those braids that robbed you of seven hours
on the eve of my departure into the 'dream' life.
Today, I am drinking cappuccino in an Internet café,
dying to create for you, a picture of the road I walk,
brushing over scores of potholes of despair
as I gasp, *show me the life in the dream.*

London life is mostly snake life. No brotherhood.
This city is a violated legend on crutches,
and this has nothing to do with rats in the tube

or fifteen-year-old gangsters prowling streets,
panthers on crack seeking 'a life of respec';
striking and avenging, cycle of bloodletting cycling on,
and on...in a land with talent for wasting lives.

As you know I did not come here to snap pigeons,
or attempt suicide by nasty Autumn breezes
that have found their way up my trousers.
Baby, I miss you. I miss you more now I realise
I don't know exactly why I came here,
constipating my stormy thirties down gullets
of English water closets, searching London's grumpy
old eyes for twinkles to misunderstand as promise.

I head butt and scream at a brick wall,
show me the life in the dream.

3

Give this message to yourself
good thing you know I am well and free
no need to say I've gone searching for gold in Timbuktu
more like Pounds in the City of London.
You may blame me for keeping you guessing
for keeping you hanging on for a decade.
I wouldn't have if I did not think it would be alright
but now you must move on, go on, to somebody new.
I must stay back and fight till I have victory.
Whatever victory I claim in the end, I still lose.

The End.

Linus Lyszkowska

THE HEALERS
(for Alexander)

In the aftermath of the 2010 Haitian earthquake,
an army of volunteers from across the world
worked miracles. People of all ages caught
in the devastation of the catastrophic quake,
bewildered, damaged in mind and body,
taken care of, tended, nurtured;
selflessly, without any expectation of reward,
those saviours helped repair the broken people,
helped them rebuild their lives, their homes,
their futures.

A 13-year-old boy in far-away England,
watching the stories unfold on television,
moved by what he has witnessed,
the unceasing care and understanding
given by these volunteers to thousands of
homeless, shocked and injured souls,
vows that he, too, one day, must become
a carer, a doctor, perhaps even a surgeon,
a healer of lives.

Lesley Burt

YOUR CHILD

You, barely beyond childhood yourself,
with peachy, unlined skin,
delighted with the plump baby in your lap;

teaching him about the scent of flowers,
conversation, play; he,
alert to your every expression.

Prophesies cannot prepare you.
After the lynching, you cradle dead weight
and remember moments like these.

(After La Madonna dei Garofani, Raphael c.1506 National Gallery, London)

K.V. Skene

TALKING TO THE DEAD

Always there is meaning, there is love

and I dream her   deft hands
at the upright   her lullabies
heavy-lidding my eyes,   her whispers
easing summer night-sounds,
winter asthma   before

she stepped into that taxi   waving goodbye

And mouths to drink the sky and tongues for singing

and nightmares of falling   off the edge
of coldblooded mornings, of ...   *Do other motherless children shiver*
through so many deciduous days, weeks, months ...?
How gone she is – how
never returning ...

Bypassing the borders of common sense and sensibility

thinking as a child I talk to her   (infant tongued)
scribble messages on the backs of old envelopes,
the margins of books – chart the minefield
of adolescence   of ways of becoming ...
still on the answerphone, her voice
from a heaven just as honest as it is hidden.

Barely aware of the ghost of a change

I stumble into an adulthood
so solid, so absolute   *The shape of my hand echoes her hand,*
minus her flat gold wedding band,
her polished fingernails ...

anchoring my overwrought, under-
exercised self I forget
those spirit-whisperings   *a mother*
        somehow labelled
        other...

All such choices can be dangerous

      as if the circling stars conspire to foreclose the future, as if
a dizziness of molecules, atoms, electrons, quarks
compels otherworlders to gatecrash *that house on Park Street I tore*
          apart, erasing every trace
          of children, husband, me
          still holds the sound of glass
          shattering, as if
our up-to-date relabellings permit a reversion
to an incurious collection of particles wanting/
waiting to be noticed

As I come out in darkness and in silence

        I can only say I was there at the first death
and cried for us all   for the whole mad/bad/radical
          habituation of a lifetime
as spirit slips from a beloved body ...   Don't look back –
the grateful dead *(still alive*
in another happier medium)   thrum the psyche,
          search for breath-shriven vocals,
witness the half-sleep of séance,
the unspeakable secrets of children ...

Beth Somerford

NO LONGER A CHILD

In the photograph your mother keeps
you look older, sporting do-it logos,
fingering the explosive rosary of
your heavy sash - its grinning teeth
and your eyes, glinting.
Here the roadsides are peppered with mines
and in one clock-tick last week
a stranger's shrapnel shucked
the tender mollusc in your head;
left it gaping.

Eilidh Thomas

MALALA DREAMS

… of a thousand friendly faces
and senses new uplifts in thermals of air

Her life glows in a limelight
of borderline as she wakes

Hold hands with Malala
she has a cloud street of stories to share

She is your mother
your sister, your daughter, you…
and a cumulus of women

Whispers of camaraderie swirl around her
blow those whispers into howling gales
release them into free convection

She is your tipping point
your conscience for resistance
your resolve, your hope…

The air is flowering
where Malala dreams

Ututu Emmanuel

ALWAYS PREYED

With strength as dormant as a Mauna Kea
Volcano, the weakest isn't a complete
Haven of weakness, otherwise
No event walked up the trigger
To make questions pop out
Like popcorns from its popper,

Then I was a prey and your best
Game: hunting, and I always
Prayed for you in every burrow
I holed up in, even when my
Breath was all the whisper
I could utter that almost

Gave my position away
Like a gift from Santa,
I still prayed; always
Like come back in a
Soccer game, I think
We enjoyed a little

Sea-saw game and we're now
Standing at the junction
Where the sinner and God
Meet; always you're the
Sinner but am not God, you're
Asking for mercy like you're

Choking for breath and expecting
Default answers but am not God,
I don't know how to play him
Like you did but if forgiveness
Will exist beyond the gates
Death, I don't want us to

Die, I pray we live forever
To see your guilt flourish like
The flowers of the field
During spring and conscience
Prick you like a nurse in need
Of blood sample but never

Getting enough until
You have lost enough
To fall into unconsciousness slowly, and
You can see me as a blurred
Ghost trailing off like smoke and
Praying you will survive.

Roger Elkin

THROUGH A GLASS DARKLY

If you were in Bosnia,
  and had followed the Neretva river
  northeast from its coastal outlet at Opuzen,
  through its broad valley, and, twisting by
  the Croatian border control, slipped due north
  past Melkovic and Klepci, across its arable plateau,
  its rich pasture, and snaked between wrecked settlements -
  Buna, Jasenica, Rodoc - with tumbled-down houses,
  gutted huts, farmlands wasted, destroyed
  and on, up through burnt-out Mostar, its broken-backed bridge,
  and beyond, as far – even – as war-torn Sarajevo
  you would question, wouldn't you, how could there be a God
  up there, looking down, allowing this to happen

        the farmer, his wife,
        their farmhands with bucket and scythe
        scattered about the yard

        cattle flattened on their sides
        and littered across ground

        chickens/ducks flustered to nothingness,
        horses toppled, sheep beached,
        the only thing on four legs, a dog

        cowsheds wrecked,
        shippon, barn, farmhouse – all upkeeled –
        their doors ajar, windows done-in, roofs tumbled

        fields displaced, even cabbage patch askew
        as if picked up and dashed back down again

hedges and fieldwalls ransacked at zagging angles,
gates unswung, trees wanting limbs

tractor abandoned, over-turned,
its driver vanished away

But this is Wales, is Bridgend, decades later,
and, Gulliver-tall, I'm this moment's divinity
blandly overviewing the crash-bang-disaster
of two-year-old grandson Adam's
cast aside Happy Valley farm

and can't help smiling wryly
at how soon we put away childish things …

Joe Fearn

NEWS REPORT FROM A NORTHERN TOWN

Heroic tales of

children,
their coats as goalposts
with the score at seventeen twelve

their fathers
stepping off the pit cage
after breathing the air the Romans breathed,

have been postponed
due to the wrong people owning the family silver.

A spokesperson said
practices they can't condone but understand
can happen, *did* happen,

they have a posh witness in a classic car
and they are standing by him.

Patrick B. Osada

LAST REUNION

Each evening, when the August sun was low,
They'd come to check the field behind the house –
Impatient for the harvest to be done.

They'd circle, honking, just above the ground
And, when the crop was in, on stubble field
Touched down in ones and twos, small family groups,

Skeins, silhouetted by the setting sun.
Leaving each morning, they'd return at dusk
For a noisy reunion every day…

And every year the pattern was the same :
They'd stay a week or so and then move on
To over-winter many miles away.

This year, when geese had gone, men came with plans :
Theodolites cast shadows over land.

Jehanne Mehta

SEA RIDERS

Araf
araf
araf nawr
slow
slow
slow down now.
Stand... stop... before this wide
blue-green expanse of ocean.
Sefwch yma
wait here, stop
at the edge,
until you feel
the rolling rhythm of the tides,
these returning cosmic cycles
that nothing interrupts,
these rolling rhythms that mould us
soul deep.
Foot falling in the sand,
feel the salt lick of the
running wave.
Listen to the
mounting roar and sink
of incoming swell,
the withdrawing rattle of sliding
shingle.
Watch the dipping wing
of kittiwake and guillemot
tumbling among these dark and massy cliffs,
where seals sing in hidden
clefts, dolphins dive, and the air stings,

sharp against your mouth,
gaping and amazed before this
ocean mystery.

Ignore the man-made clouds that
stripe the sky,
dropping steely rods of rain, deploying drought,
like armaments, displacing
the habitual patterns of
wind and weather: sorcerer's apprentice stuff this, which
we are bound to drown in,
when fear takes over,
feeding on surface insecurity.

But no.
Ar agor.
Open,
we are open,
open for business
with a deeper magic,
allied
to the unstoppable rhythm
of the tides.

We are sea riders,
riders of the deep.

Vanessa Gebbie

CARRAIG AN AIFRINN

The sign to the Mass Rock
was pushed round its post by the lads,
and now it points vaguely towards Eyeries village
and O'Sullivan's shop: purveyors
of grocery, hardware and petrol.

But in a way it doesn't matter,
for who am I or they to say
that Mass may not be said somewhere
between the shampoo and the shrink-wrapped cheddar,
the bin bags and sprays
for black spot on the roses?

So let us give thanks
that the Redcoats will not be
flinging open the door any time soon,
sending the postcard rack flying
(Eyeries, Best Kept Village, 2012),
brandishing bayonets.

Let us give thanks for
O'Sullivan's lawn and garden products,
the availability of newspapers
both local and national,
the wide range of vegetables, toys and treats.
And kindling, and all sorts of
bread, and wine.

John McCullough

TALACRE

where we turned off the dissolving path
to chance uncertain territory. High dunes

like hills of sugar, so smooth we lost whole feet
but found ourselves again, defied dense sky

by making our own light. We followed
the roaming fence and, like the rabbits

darting over marram, were never caught out.
We reached a new country, the sea

at first too far and blocked by swerving
channels – mercury in the dimness –

but we weren't afraid to innovate,
rolling up trousers for running jumps,

splatting down with a squelch to write names
in sand among the casualties

of starfish, bladderwrack. Messy letters,
our fingers digging past the first resistance,

our only witnesses the wind turbines way out –
a sleepy, inaudible crowd, two so close

to each other from our perspective, we swore
they must have occupied the same dream.

Helen Moore

MONSOON JUNE

*After the Christian Aid advert depicting a South Asian woman up to
her neck in water, with the caption — Do us a favour will you? Write
to your MP about that climate change bill!*

The water's encircling my neck, Kali –
a damp strangle like the hands of my brother,
when he's too drunk to know better.
And these rags I called a sari
are wings trailing in these fields-turned sea
that flap me up to rooftops, bridges
where we perch with our dry-lipped children, waiting.

Sometimes when darkness laps at our feet
and the Moon throws us silver shackles,
I lie awake, wishing your four arms would pincer me away,
prize my skull among the garlands
that chatter from your breasts
as you dance the charnel-grounds with Lord Shiva.

But I must be strong for all our little ones;
and so each day I wade with my hollow-bellied vessel –
like a girl trying to swim, her float so buoyant – praying
you'll speed my return – the long, long way from the pump,
clean water leaden on my head.

The stench I can accept, the bloated corpses, flooding
sewage – but keep those scaly Muggers snoozing in their lairs
now their hunting grounds are everywhere.
And yes, I do seek protection, dear Durga,
though I've made no offerings – the usual ball of rice
and flowers – but we have nothing now,
and the plants are drowned.

Archana says the villages of Maharashta come last
for handouts because the newsmen never visit –
they stay in Mumbai where sacred Cows
are floating in the streets.

The holy men believe these are the heaviest rains
India's known in all her history –
in the city many houses have no light, telephone, or water
from the tap. And so perhaps we're lucky?
When rains sweep the world away,
we know how to live on the edge.

Kate Firth

CRACKINGTON HAVEN ON NEW YEARS' EVE

At the twist of the year, watching the whirl
of the world on the cliffs, a chaos of waves
flail in the sky, as the heavens weave
pearly curls of ivory. This storm
is skirring your ragged December

through pebbles between your feet. Bubbling
suds creep to your ankles, the ooze
sucking the scum of your failures
back to the source. From the brook by the bridge,
fresh water pumps up in funnels

to skitter a river into the salt. Watching
this meeting of waters and ferment,
you ponder the froth   unable to fathom
the moment the stream stops   being a stream
and succumbs   to a vastness of sea.

Rachel J. Fenton

OUTLIERS

Bathed in Burra Firth's foamy mouth,
Flugga's mermaid coifs
her hair aloft ophiolite rock, diabase and dark
mafic glass crackles like static in magic
light at her feet. Two giants
crashed here like her kids,

obtuse, competitive
Saxa full of confidence,
Herma, better-lived: the only ones who told her they loved
her. Long gone,
they're sleeping now on lava
pillows. Silly buggers,

they couldn't see
she was dragging them down with her. *Blows*:

Out Stack and Muckle Flugga; the emoticon
for kiss is the same as it is for bitter. So south
of the far north, the sea, too, cries with laughter.

Lin Lundie

FLOOD

Salt water flows back
through ancient ryfes and ditches

the old house dries out
in the opening air of windows and doors
a mild spring
a sense of relief
a washing away.

She knew change was coming –
it was in the air, in her bones.

Light hearted, grateful for the warning,
the reminder of impermanence,
she packs away family treasures
for grandchildren, for whoever will care,
gives away clothes, clears cupboards, empties
drawers of heavy linen, dusty papers,
walls and ceilings have layers
of whitewash, curtains washed
and shrunk, hang back at windows.

Old furniture, dried and cracked
with witness marks to its history,
is polished with beeswax and lavender.

She feels its smooth boards under her hands
wonders who would own it next.

A new start then,
or the end of the past.
She will open the place to summer's heat,
bring in flowers, roses, branches
from the olives.
She will stay,
be in the sigh and slap
of the sea's breathing,
need to stand outside
with a whirl of swallows above

need to feel his length
stretched lean against her in the morning,
walk the sand in the dawn,
be the grey cat.

Love, she knows, is the low turn
in the tide, silver, shimmering
smooth as a starched linen sheet
or wild, when the wind gets up,
knots and tangles all careful
arrangements
needing nothing much except

time perhaps

time to put flowers in pots and jars,
watch them fade,
do it again,
watch the egret in the shallows,
relearn the art of standing still
breathing
till the leaves fall.

Diana Mitchener

OMENS

'I'm taking a gap year.' A silence fell.
'Travelling with friends to Thailand and beyond.'
The elders' eyes lost focus, faces stilled.

I sat cross-legged, defiant.   Father rose
took down Old Moore's Almanac,
turned pages, sucked his teeth,
                                    and frowned.

Mother collected piles of yarrow stalks,
counted out fifty, then set one aside,
divided forty nine into two parts,

counted and divided, counted, divided,
following oriental rituals
till twenty six remained.
                    She shook her head.

Grandmother muttered in the tool shed
fingering the bloodied entrails of a stoat
spilling their secrets on her open palm.
She pressed a talisman into my hand.

My Aunt consulted the *I Ching,* threw coins
six times: two for a head, three for a tail;
drew up a hexagram: *K'an K'an: 'The abyss,*

Misfortune. Water above, below.
Nine at the beginning means
danger, destruction, death.'
                    I scoffed.

I hurled the Almanac into the wheelie bin,
flung coins and yarrow stalks into the brook,
told Grandmother her entrails were disgusting.
Shouted it was my choice, my right to go.

They stood like gravestones at the terminal.
Flight 926. The wind
rippled the rain across the tarmac.

                              A wave.

And the tsunami came as Father had foretold.

Whole towns collapsed. Planks
strewn like yarrow stalks swirled,
sub-divided into driftwood piles.
Bodies like drowned stoats stink along the shore.

And I sit cross-legged, grieving on the sand,
clutching the talisman,
counting loss on loss.

Mario Petrucci

THIS NIGHT GARDEN &

the way august heat in the skull draws in its own
kind of shadow around a remembered house stilling to blur
beyond borders the chiaroscuro blooms of what

days are – till blood in its quieter hours begins
to hear far off in itself through that fragrance after yesterdays'
rain a refrain rhythmically soft as a child's as

if sound were a window thrown open to cool
& boundless sadness billowing sight so of a sudden one might
sense an edge to everything human some

-how somewhere where single lives are
each a note passed over in their lullaby lilted once & once
only before sleep : a man again a boy

a woman once more a girl who each
ghost down adjacent stairs in adjacent houses afraid
to wake unaware how the other in

crush for them has come into mid-
summer into a garden where heat's blister flares
heads between legs with thought

a form of longing & longing that
smallest boat urged out into slopping-black
water – each listening for what

pours in from above : the surge
deep from zinc sparks so far so utterly
still yet pitched as love is

tiniest light from twin motes
a child alone in love can just make
out & not that sweetest

dark so darkly sweet between

Tania Hershman

THE WEIGHT OF US

As I line up to board my flight
I see the pilot

lean out and wipe his window
with what looks like

a tissue. Surrounded
by technology, I find something

reassuring in that sight: the man
charged with the weight

of us, trusting nothing
            but his own hand.

A C Clarke

THE CHOICE

Do it again?
Step off into
air, no safety net
trusting in who knows what
to bear me up?

There was a moment -
of glitter, threadbare velvet,
cheap perfume –
I could have turned away.
I looked in the foxed mirror

touched up lipstick
stepped over
the line. I did not know
how it would feel
to be in freefall, the mind

plummeting. I did not know
I would end up a ghost
or how love corked in a bottle
flung far as could be
for time to carry away

would come back waterlogged,
uneasily remembered,
like this photo smiling up
from the drawer
where its edges curl.

Roselle Angwin

BUDDHA GARDEN, GARDOUSSEL

I won't say that even in paradise
there is a snake
but I will say that even in this garden
death too has its dwelling-place –
the butterfly knocked by careless feet
whose wings can no longer bear its weight
the plump vole in the tortoiseshell cat's teeth
the little and greater losses we admit to
in each of our own life's orbit –

Last night in the perfect wooded hills
against a perfect twilit sky
la chasse began, and the shots
seemed to ricochet off every tree
until the whole great bowl
of the valley fractured and cracked
could no longer hold

And below something in me broke too
at another absence at a human hand
another tear in the weave of things –
the rip now that had been a deer, and again a deer
and a boar – great savage chasms
opening at the edges of this our more-than-human family
and into which each of us also must fall.

Jackie Wills

DAY OF REST

The order comes: "Down tools."
You stop driving buses, lock the tills.
Guides leave the Taj Mahal,
Pyramids. Ski lifts hang over glaciers.
In markets, all you hear is flies –
there's no-one underground, no planes,
no money moves. TVs show blue lagoons
to a soundtrack of wind. Food's eaten raw.
Your tongue remembers the taste of blood,
your hand how an apple gives as you pull
it from a tree. Dancing returns to empty
spaces the way a cactus blooms.
You watch a wren, look up to the sky
you fell from. You become the greeting
of a Venda woman: "Ah," a slow exhalation.

Helen Clare

FIGS

The sticky wizened sacs of Christmases past,
the brown inside fig rolls – the 'piggies' I mashed
with half cut milk teeth. They are hotel breakfasts
alongside tinned grapefruit and reconstituted prunes.

I have never seen them like this, soft and fresh
and never cut into one. It has creamy flesh
and a deep pink flower inside. Bisected
it is a tree, a womb, a heart, a hand, a world.

And so it is, that the fig wasp nibbles a hole
through fruit to the flower, into which she must crawl
carrying pollen, sometimes laying her eggs
and sometimes dying there, tangled in the seeds.

Years ago, a Pashtun boy told me that a modest woman
was like a fig, the flower of her beauty hidden
beneath the soft folds of her dark clothes
Now, an Iraqi woman tells me of a house

with a garden, with a tree heavy with gold-skinned
fruit that she picked each morning. I'm ashamed
that I am too squeamish to eat such beauty. I wonder
if Iraq too is like a fig, and what would be the flower

at the fruits core, what the gold or darkened shroud
who would pollinate and who would only feed.
I push for a while to build a metaphor
but know at heart a fig is just a fig, and war is war.

Anna Lunt

FATHERS AND SONS

The sins of the fathers are visited upon
Their children to the third generation.
Thus, each one of us is born
Unto our certain crucifixion;

And each must struggle through existence.
Yet, heaven upon earth is only ever just three generations hence
And one lifetime could be enough
To see the world abound in love.

*

Lamenting the news
As war continues,
Within my heart a flower of solace blossoms:
My sons will not take up arms.

Those to whom I gave birth
Will not be the agents of death.
Those to whom I gave life
Will not be the cause of another mother's grief.

Shirley Wright

ARÊTE *

Ahead, the final slog up Striding Edge
to the summit. His feet throb inside boots
laced clumsily, though tight enough
to hold his heart together. Blisters burn his heels
and he'll suffer tomorrow. 360 degrees show
green like oxygen, grassy rain-rich green

so unlike Helmand's scorched terrain that green
exists as if for the first time. At the edge
of memory a crump of gunfire, a show
of red in dust where he left an arm, his combat boots
and hope ground to grit beneath the heel
of wrong time, wrong place, but luck enough

to make it back. In his rucksack enough
mintcake to feed an army. However green
he may be to fell-walking, some part of heel
and toe knew to haul him to this rough edge.
Poets used to climb here often, boots
pounding syllables out of muddy grass to show

that words can lurk in dirt. Now it's his show,
though a one-handed pianist has little enough
to offer. But first, the OS trig point, then boots
off and food. Plodding on, he's gulping green
by the lungful while in his head a riff whose funky edge
is all his own. By the cairn he stops to eat, a heel

of bread and cheese and yet more pills to heal
the stump. What really hurts doesn't show –
missing fingertips twitching him to the edge.

Weapons into words, he wonders, might that be enough;
rhythm and rhyme, the march of metric feet, a green
gage summer with his heart no longer in his boots?

He stands, untethered, on Helvellyn's edge, boots
discarded, facing the sheer drop, wind wild enough to heel
him over into the buzzard's flighty show, out into green.

A sharp ridge, a high rocky edge on a mountain

Norbert Hirschhorn

SYRIA, 2015

Look, Damascus will cease to be a city,
will become a heap of ruins (Isaiah 17:1)

Beelzebub, your host of flies
Drink tears from babies' eyes
Carry shit from drainage ditches
Dysentery and scabrous itch
Flies that feed – black, carrion, horse
Flies on shrouds, on bridal corpse
Midges piercing gauzy mesh
Botfly maggots in festering flesh
Drones that buzz before you die
O! loathsome Lord of Flies,
Death begets rebirth:
Your acolytes shall inherit the earth

Caroline Davies

AMBUSH

You are back in jungle heat.
But the man who walks
        towards you from the mirror
looks strangely old.
Shouldn't you be wearing what remains
        of your uniform?

The others are not frightened.
The museum attendants in grey shirts
            are here to help.
They are not guards.

Even the pebbled flints
        could be a beach,
not rocks you have to break.

Sit down on the stones,
            and listen for the sea.
But still you tremble
until a small boy with fair hair
        swings his magic torch
to light the ceiling's sky
        with a pattern of stars.

Nick Cooke

HIGH WOOD

I

A shell fit for bursting
to reveal what –
shrapnel or embryo
in a mangled copse?

And always that grimace
as the known world changes,
the lumpen horde crouching,
fat digits in stony ears.

Now the newborn grapples forth,
the shell is a parapet,
and none round here pays mind
to horizons booming.

II

Primrose won't cut it
nor marigold either
nor even the brightest halo
in Giotto's egg tempera.

No, I need yellow
like you never yellowed it before
to do my art justice
and catch the newborn heaving

out over twigs and brambles,
the barbed wire of the trees.
Worth your salt are you,
O kingly paint-maker?

Then make that salt so white
it sears the even whiter eyeballs
and if I want snow on those trees –
or the battle-ploughed earth –

burn me God's magnesium, let the viewer
flinch, recoil, turn away half-blind.
I don't aim to be looked at.
I seek to be remembered.

III

For infant, soldier, artist,
the world tumbles slower,
a grinding take, frame by sepia frame,
on what the butler or the general saw.

Observe me here, squatting
astride my time-bomb installation.
Can't you hear the cogs turn?
Did you see the shutter click?

My point, precisely.
It's a good while since you slipped
the wreckage of the nest,
your hands smooth as tulips.

Jean–Mark Sens

SEPTUAGENARIANS

In the early morning, the septuagenarians pass by the house
they walk as men carrying their bodies under obligations
slight oscillations of their heads, steps partially balanced
        in pensiveness
the clumsiness of the flesh in between refusal and resignation,
        aging and duress
they pass mostly unlooking, a sparse procession,

each on the regulations of prescribed and tailored
        medical regiments.
The street in recovery of digs and road works
the city's guts exposed
lines, conduits for draining, channels, culverts
underground furrows of its life support.

You sit on the porch to befriend this small rural, ensconced
        city over the Gulf of Mexico
maybe read a line or two, splicing some from your own
        imaging in between news
trying to put the broadest of the sea, close yet invisible, in
        your mind
its nearby smell purporting the vision of the poked
        face wetlands
the coastline necklaces of oyster shells and berms
and the workforce on the beach fanning across the sand
decontamination suits to clean what spewed from the
        gouged seafloor.
Some New York lawyer in want of sorrow and pity
the locals heard Mr. Compensation can turn compassion
        into cash,
the odor of the crude not so sweet

tar balls rolling on the shore like black urchins
brown pelicans in crows' togas playing a dead ballet
over the shore.
Tomorrow the septuagenarians will pass by, I never count
their number,
the after-life a greater stride beyond the infinite of the
perfect resurfaced avenue
satori, Jesus, or nirvana, and not to wonder why.

Wendy Klein

THE WORD FOR *LOST* IN SWAHILI

Find your phone found you this morning on a road
not far from the Burundi National Park,

so minute on my screen, I zoomed and zoomed
to see it before it moved off again in the direction

of Kyabamba, where there are volcanoes (live?)
and not far off, Lake Edward, its name printed out

in both English and French, but the nearby
Ugali River Game Reserve will offer its own

temptations – lions, elephants, rhinos, long-lashed
giraffes – do not be seduced, so many beasts,

dangerous, endangered. But I see you're moving
again: Musama, Kigoma, Tabora, where the search

widens, hones in on Rwanda, Burundi, a recital
of massacres, and across the map, Beni, Butembo .

Where are you going my heart? Ivy is rampaging
everywhere; it's choking the wild cherries

and blossoms are falling from your plum tree,
though your apple is still in flower.

If you're lost will your phone find you? Do you
know the word for *lost* in Swahili?

My bed is unruffled; I am sleeping
too well without you.

Thomas R. Smith

MONARCH WITH A TORN WING
For Scott King

The Monarch fluttered awkwardly
on wet pavement. We noticed
a small tear in one of its wings,
feared it might be hopelessly injured.
But I got it to climb on my finger
with its black eyelash feet and lifted
it onto the head-high branch of a maple
on the boulevard. At least there
it would have a better death than
down where foot traffic could crush it. . . .

Monarchs are fewer. I've seen only
two or three so far this summer.
My worry was more for the species
than the individual. Later Krista asked
Scott if a butterfly could still fly
with a torn wing. My publisher is also
a naturalist. "Absolutely. Often
they're ripped by birds or other insects."
He'd seen one with all its orange lost, yet
aloft. I remembered how when we'd passed
the maple again, the Monarch was gone.

Richard Skinner

THE DIVINE CORTEX

At dusk, she walked along the wire fences
and saw a hole in the ground.
She thought of her grandfather, speechless
since his fall into a crater.

She imagines his silence at seeing the fire,
blooming like a flower,
at smelling the soft musk of explosions.

THE INEVITABLE ACCUMULATION OF DETAIL

She dreamt of blue electricity, one dark night,
fizzing through her eyes and head.

The next evening, she walked
along the city river and comprehended the streetlights.
She looked at the dark sky and heard the trill
of young, white stars. She looked deeper and made out the hum
of stars older and red.

Richard Skinner

MATTERS IRIE

Serge drove his cart every morning delivering milk. He talked
to his customers about astronomy and the weather.
One fine morning, his legs scissored and he collapsed —
a window in the street cracked and the sun went in.

His daughter, Cecile, stayed by his bed for three days.
On the fourth, a doctor showed her the X-rays. He pointed,
but she couldn't tell if the grey area was a tumour, a rainstorm
     or a galaxy.

APHASIA

As the train moved, the old man opposite him looked out the
     window
and tapped his hearing aid all night.

Next morning, the old man is gone.
He looks out and sees the horizon always receding, he tries to
     imagine
what the old man saw.
He forgets that the world is only his mind
gone mad with remembering.

Roger Elkin

THEIR THRESHOLD

For James and Helen

I   *Not* The Italian Job

He comes in a tad sheepishly, eyes fixed
yet certain and obviously troubled despite
the brave face he's putting on; and, as if
to prove it, clutching this sheaf of internet
printouts, double-spaced, numbered and stapled.

Knowing him, we know it's bound to be
full of instruction expressed in layman's terms:
what's to be done, by whom, when,
at what time-duration, with what consequences,
the outcomes, expectations and results,
the technological-cum-scientific jargon and data,
the precise technical terminology and application
all tamed to emasculation, and unthreatening.

So we're not surprised when pointing
to the printout he says quietly, dispassionately

> *The way forward, this. The only way.*
> *Zap it. Zap. And we bounce back. We'll*
> *get through. Time on our side. Work or*
> *not, what's money anyway. Just hold it*
> *in balance, so don't go over the edge.*
> *It's all in here. Zap it. And wait. Wait …*

He takes a breath; steps nearer; back;
near again; then almost apologetically
hands us the printout booklet

with its bland announcement:
Hodgkin's Lymphoma

and we know that from now on
we're living his cliff-hanger for real.

II   **Neck Lump**

Felt it before she saw it, fingers
lingering as circling its rise and swell,
then pincering but not pinching skin,
just sensing, as if testing whether
there was any give in it. Certainly nothing
she could name as hurt or pain, but a dulled
muscle-pull, or under-bruise, barely there.
Not much to worry about, she thought,
though mirrors confirmed she'd better
have it checked.

                  And did.

The excision would leave its giveaway
snail trail: that thinned down carmine pink
she could conceal behind filigree chain
whose intricate links would divert looks,
bring praise
             or, for special days, a garlanded
scarf wreathed in practised casualness
and satisfying others' eyes
                    unless, of course,
she really felt the need to advertise how she'd
survived the lump, the knife, the chemo-fix

then she'd plump for going open-necked,
a defiant, self-confessing cut above the rest.

Margaret Wilmot

THE NON-ENTOMBMENT OF THE FOX

The full moon glances over a splayed body,
dark hole in the fox's chest. In the washed field his weight
is a black hole, matter collapsed.
The belly's white hovers, separates –
as in the *Entombment* where Titian frames the corpse
with pale streaks of winding-sheet and cloud.
(The men struggling to convey their Lord
have ruddy arms and garments rich as blood.)

I kneel beside the still, fur-fangled self. Yearn
to ease his earthed soul on its way. Yearn
for his rebirth. The moon pulls, and air
sheer as light breathes round us everywhere.
Life is all-pervasive in the atmosphere.
Soon the fox will disappear.

Caron Freeborn

RAGS AND BONES

He pushed the wheelbarrow towards her.
Look, he said, an old hose,
wormed into holes. Here's a lock of my
bike, and a collapsing brick. See that sweet
grain? A map of its world.
Oh, the deep loneliness of things.
A rusted bucket. A step, untrodden,
a shuttered eye. An iron pause.
Here, he said, these are for you.

You will love them, call them, so they are yours.
Yes, she said, running her hands along
filings until they splintered her palms
with savage intensity. Yes, I'll sleep
with you now.

Caroline Maldonado

PAGES

1.

An old woman reads.
Light from her book illuminates
her face, all else

falls away into darkness.
A shawl pulled round her shoulders
protects her from the outside world.

She wants nothing of it.
She wants to live in her book.

2.

The bookstore stays open all night. You can read there as long
as you like.

Early arrivals take the few chairs and sofas, someone is lodged in
every corner, readers stretch their long limbs into the corridors,
an elderly man is lying in a hammock slung from a beam – all
you can see is the round weight of his body & the veins flowing
like ink over the hand holding up the book.

Here's a girl with her boyfriend. Now he, now she, turns the
page & you can see how they love what they read by their fit,
one enclosed in the arm of the other, the gaps between them
growing smaller by the hour.

As the light comes up & the bars along the street begin to close,
all of them leave – how many there are! – & walk out into the
city.

3.

They're off – the neighbour's children
kitted out in red and blue

chill air against hot cheeks –
remember that weightless feeling?

He slowly puts down his book
turns away from the window

as the February sky rears
towards him in full spate.

4.

'...but it *isn't* life.
It lacks flesh, lacks blood'.

5.

A man (who as a child living in poor rural Basilicata had to read
by candle-light when it grew dark) filled his 3-wheeled motor
with old books & set up a mobile library for his village,
but soon – in response to demand from other villages
– he needed to travel further & further collecting
& lending books & that required a larger motor
which he decked out like a house
with front door & windows
even a chimney.

6.

Monastic scribes lit their pages
with burnished gold leaf
on vellum and therein

manus scriptum sang their gospels
while monsters of evil and chaos
danced in the margins.

7.

Waters still race in the rivers that drove the papermills
of Pioraco.

8.

Her tablet, abandoned on the table
trembles and grows dark.

Sleepy on the sofa, the girl
tucks in her legs and rests her head
on her folded arm.

I can't see her face
see whether she's smiling.

Caron Freeborn

THEME PARK

M-i-c-k-e-y M-o-u-s-e
we chant, queued behind the woman with fat
arse flood-swelled out of blue rayon pants; sat
next to her, in its bloated pram, we see
her child, half-faced, tooth split and spiking free
as though skin were soft as spit. My child taps
my arm thin, hides his sweet wholeness, trapped by
facing fear he's told – that's me – he's wrong to feel.
For my child is deficient. Mentally.
He is, it says so on his special pass.
Twenty-first century freak-show boy, he
self-displays: see the plinth-disordered brain,
less than you, than me. Is she physically
deficient, that girl? She's just goofy with pain.

Nick Cooke

THIRTY-ONE

Look at me now, plunging
through all kind of undergrowth:
beacons aglare, my tail a blistery comet.

Nothing in this domain is a match
for the coiled cat power
I pack in each shoulder blade,
the tide of bone over joint.

And sometimes we get to handle
the overgrowth too. Just last week
a brother jumped the cage

and hit the genocide memorials
of Phnom Penh, mocking his keepers.
As always we divide the nation -
the outraged, the pragmatic -

but what think ye now,
you thirty beside me? Do we play it
head down and thank our lucky bars,

or heed our blood to the end,
battering a path from all corners,
daring them to draw and quarter
on the unsurrendered plain?

Mario Petrucci

BLEAK BLOOD

Bleak blood we've bled through the eyes, down our cheeks
and yet nothing is seen. No flood alarm, no tidal warning.

Deep in our heart-chambers hatched smooth stones of love.
If their bold mother flies into storm, so must the fledglings.

We lowered faces into dust at the edge of the path the Friend
frequents, rewarded by dust if dust is what the Friend leaves.

Our weeping is a torrent that seizes even the stoniest heart,
tumbling it down these stairs of land, drunkenly out to sea.

How can I thirst, then, when I am this awash with myself?
I burst my dam to splash Your road, the hem of Your robe.

In envy, sunset shreds kindly clouds because my Moon has
swooned and roundly, whitely weaves for me a coat of light.

In the Wine-house street, this heart now pounds a purer beat:
it is a Sufi dancing here in my convent, gently, like a prayer.

Spencer Edgar

EBOLA

Oh ancient ancestor,
Our true progenitor,
Make yourself known!
Live amongst us,
So we may see your power.

Drink deeply from our impotence,
So we may remember our heritage
Of ivory and human trade.
Eat of our flesh and sinew
Our very essence you begat,
When all was one and singular,
Before tissue, bone and gristle.

Simple protein, archaic wonder,
Of a world beyond ancient,
Who bows to no law of evolution.
Parasite, saprophyte,
Survivor on the fittest.

Who created you?
Surely no merciful creator,
No instructions to submit,
To human dominion.
Yes, we were given the sky,
The ocean and the land,
To protect and coral,
But your intelligent design,
Outwits our minds,
In simple natural murder.

We raise our flags,
And mark our borders.
We exploit our neighbours,
And rattle our sabres.
We plough our land,
And mine our minerals.
Yet you sweep it aside,
Your invisible hostility,
Mining our vitality,
Ploughing our bodies,
Back Into the burnt earth.

You, of the primordial forest,
Dormant in the dark heart,
Hibernating in the tropical heat,
Living amongst mammals,
who dine on grains and fruit.
Hosting a killer, a volcano,
Rising up, multiplying,
Pouring out of the jungle cauldron,
Unstoppable!
Flowing through us, liquefying us,
Marking your path with cross after cross,
As you march relentlessly towards the sea.

Marc Woodward

PETROL STATION SITUATION

He joked with her
across the car roof
while he fiddled with the keys.
Under his arm a road atlas.
He with shirt tails
hanging and She
in a winter coat.

She laughed a slight laugh
and looked down,
waiting for the catch.
Happy to be going
somewhere together.

On a cold forecourt
I only saw their smiles
and envied their possibilities.
I didn't wonder where they were heading.

Instead I turned my key,
blinked as the sat nav
awoke,
and wondered
where I was.

Jacquie Wyatt

EGGSHELLS

How does the white feel
strained from the yolk?
A dribble of albumen
on the stained work-surface
as unset as me,
as opaquely vulnerable.

You haunt my nostrils
when I brush past
the coat you keep leaving behind.
Your bulk possesses
the mattress I don't replace
as I roll towards
your deep hollow.

When you breathed my expelled air
what of me
did you distill
and keep?

While we sleep apart
my mind scurries
across the rooftops of our lives
searching for the company
of the man you used to be.

Anne Stewart

THE SPANISH ISLANDS

"I've booked a holiday village" she says.
I see cockroaches and thieves,
lager louts abusing the pool
but say "What date do we leave?"

There's a purpose to this holiday
neither of us has spoken of.
Who speaks of broken years?
Mothers, of daughters lost?

I look up local festivals and foods,
advice for tourists, hire a car.
She buys new crossword books
and tops her list with decks of cards.

And that first night, the rhythmic
wash of sea interrogating land
will tiptoe with us in the dark
uncertain of the shifting sand.

Charlotte Gann

OUR SHORT TIME

You come out of the station nodding at the grey bridge,
smiling. Everything unchanged except, at some point,
they painted over the graffiti – where it always said 'Bridge'

but of course we knew it was really Bridget
after Louise's mother. We walk and you tell me your story –

what those days and nights were for you, how his wardrobe

nearly broke you. You describe hanger upon hanger
of cream chinos, racks of desert boots.

By the horse-jumps you explain appreciation –
how you see things differently now. As we turn down
the broad slope, I grow terrified I won't have time to tell you.

David Caddy

DEFUSION

Scar tissue beside nerve track
water spread wider in fits.
Shill bank saturated silt,
Mill slip, diversely bereft.

Forty years on and the eddies by
Inkpen's Hole underwhelm.
Broken reeds, rush and grass,
Stur current, fail to cleft the storm.

Upstream pollutants, wrist
patted, as anything goes.
Edenic trees, orchard, hedgerow
bees, up and left by haze.

Owner, tenant, stuck in quicksand
to the point that waste becomes
norm and effort too great a risk as if
all was lost to death and eternal flow.

River bed undredged, subsidies
unclaimed, implants pharmaceutically
blurred, round world of blue,
make an eye out of you.

Celia Dixie

STARLINGS

I sat in Lyons with a Bakewell tart,
Voltaire on the table. I'd hardly lived,
just read, thought, wanted.

The café clattered: metal trays, teapot lids;
silver heaters churning steam.
I didn't hear the starlings,

jostling on ledges, perched
in the canyon of Corporation Street,
above shop lights, green buses.

Now they're high in the beeches
as I hang out the washing.
I turn, the trees are bare.

Starlings stream from us like children.
Their wet cries fill my garden.

Georgi Y. Johnson

THE LIE THAT YOU ARE GONE

We would have us believe this tree,
flowering and bearing sweetest fruit
is the death knell of a seed,
that once entwined with animal fur
found home in fertile soil.

We might see an empire of clouds
reflecting every tincture of light
and decide this transient beauty
is the death chant of a river.

Perhaps we should bow to whispers
that butterflies blown through flowers
are but death knells of slugs
we tried to avoid in the mud.

And just as we hear sweet melody,
through branches of our minds,
Would we say this song is dying,
even as it is sings?

Does the silent moon decry
the death of a blazing sun?

Always ourselves arriving,
How would we lie and say
that now, you have passed?

Is a rock separate from a blade of grass?
Is it liquid, this thin shield of death,
this transparent divider of glass?

Let me in, sweet sister, to your sweetness
Let me dissolve in nectar of all you are
Let me absorb you into earthly tone
Let it come, let it be, let it be free.

Not grieving but living again
as each step to death
walks us closer to life.

Gordon Simms

ESTUARY

Soon, one of us will draw the blinds.
The fog lumbers in, grey to ivory,
and the moment will arrive, a point
of balance when the balcony
glides, its rail a departing ferry
or a slipway loping into dusk.

Almost a week since the cloud
swam down to claim its river: day
inches in behind schedule, leaves early.

And soon, when one of us can wait no longer,
we'll slide the curtains close,
jettison whatever's left out there
and estimate the nearest reference
to where we think we are,
in the dark, inside.

Jan Harris

SURPRISING TIMES

We devour the day like a scrumped apple,
sincerely note a lessening of gravity. It seems
the tufted duck floats inches above deep water
but she merely stands in the shallows.
A devious wind upturns a swan
his rubber foot treads the air then stretches.

Rain is forecast, yet dry leaves fall on our heads,
scrunched letters from lost days.
We expected russet, gold, ochre, vermillion;
there is brown and brown and a small boy
proudly bearing a hundred spring green leaves.
Rumpled sheep sit cross legged on benches

and our reflections in the lake laugh
and laugh at the absurdity of making plans.

Celia Dixie

BOA

I saw it through the frosted glass
of the front door, a ruffled band
of black beneath her tilted chin.

She took her thin coat off, but kept
the boa at her neck, glittering
in the firelight, till it slithered

to the floor and coiled itself there.
The cat came, eyeing it, picking
his way to the fire. She warmed

her hands, spreading her fingers
like bony wings, reaching for words,
searching the flames.

That night she cried out in her dreams.
By morning she was sleeping
as she used to, open-limbed.

Downstairs, the cat slipped past me.
I found feathers by the hearth,
restored to the spirit of birds.

Rose Flint

RUNNING ON EMPTY

I ran from my Mother before I was born
(and she'd tried so hard, made me of star-ash, clay, rain)
but I raced downtown and went chasing the easy speedy
routes over fields of fuel (feet dirty, heart hungry)
trawling the wide mouth of my Fendi sack for spoils,
discarding and trading: *uranium, copper and cotton,*
bodies and palm oil, sugar, coffee, coal futures, gold –

Someplace I spilled babies, somewhere I drew crowds,
but I rushed on faster, eating and spitting out riches,
winding higher and higher through wasteland and mountain
until I reached the edge and stopped - with nothing before me.

Sirocco and shadow have formed the last of my family:
Grandmother Earth, stick-thin and bony, so fragile, so
easily broken; scorched, hairless, dry breasted, abraded –
Only the two of us matter, only us in existence.

I could leave her. Go on running on empty –
or take off my Prada jacket and wrap it around her,
set tinder to flame in my shoes and sit at her feet, listening
to Wisdom: the First voice of Spirit, breath of the future.

Kyle Norwood

DAY AND NIGHT

Keep repeating the same words until more come,
that's the secret to thinking. It happens slowly,
like getting out of bed one leg at a time. You hear
your thoughts echo, as if someone inside you is thinking them,
and the solution rises like a diver coming up for air.
He quietly insists upon it until you ask whether there's been
some misunderstanding, you aren't the person who was meant.
Or are you? The dim colors in the garden slosh into each other
until suddenly, without transition, there is sunlight and shadow.
Can we bear now to catch the heavy pennies as they fall,
everything we thought we wanted? Is the landscape
the right attire for the occasion, is it the moment
for handsome proposals, or is the day already too long,
does the text blur, the head fall back, and tigerfish
chase angelfish down corridors where machines revolve
all night to counterfeit the truest currency?

Linda Black

SOMEWHERE A SHELF

Spine ends sunned. Edge wear and fractional bumping to corners.

Which strategy? She suspects the alphabet. Something visual? How to remember a shopping list: Walk out of your front door (hypothetically). No sooner have you stepped out than you hear a crunching sound (1. A box of eggs.) What a mess! Never mind, down the steps, neatly tripping over an orange, three of them (Item No 2); along the path, something crisp underfoot (3.Cereal) etc. etc. Here's the drift: no nearer, no further away.

Back-strip detached from front cover. One inch of front gutter re-glued. Age-grimed.

Where could she have been! And for what purpose? She had looked and her mind had declined: Let it stay. Leave it. You have no need. Context eluding her again like a missed opportunity.

Short gift note on endpaper. No dust jacket. Numerous illustrations.

To locate again the shelf among shelves, the book among books in a room unparalleled; to lift from the shelf the cloth-backed book, to unhook it, read again the title lettered in gilt, *Things Fall Apart* ; to not put it back.

Hinges cracked. Scattered foxing to prelims, fore-edge and occasionally to pages. Contents in fine condition.

Anthony Costello

MARK ROTHKO

If the world is an adult predating on a child,
And the 'teen a manifestation
Of the child's indiscriminate revenge,
And the old, frail and flapping behind a curtain of fear,
Fearing all, even the good, the innocents,
Then let us leave the world not to the animals
(And their Darwinian devourings)
Or their insect and bacteria cousins,
Not even plant life with its cycle
of death and decaying matter

The inheritor of the Earth
The View, in and for itself,
Where sea meets sky, ice
Mountain, rock, basic landscape,
Pure lines of horizon,
Like the dreamy vistas of Ansell Adams,
The cloudscapes of Turner,
Hokusai on Fuji or Mark Rothko's
Meditation on the colour Red,

The child of the Universe
Stopped in its track of tears
By a benevolent God or any Stanley Kubrick,
Where I was always uncertain
If the oversized freakish baby
Floating through the Universe
At the end of 2001: a Space Odyssey
Was the end of humanity or the beginning,
The spent horror on every doll's face
Our childhood past, or childhood to come.

R.T. Calway

THE WHITE CHRISTMAS TREE

It appeared in November, last year's tree.
Obvious among rubble and bramble,
artificial 'frozen fir' with thin, white
needles of plastic; aluminium trunk.

It lay on its side, shed of all meaning.
Life, green life, had not been brought within halls
but lifelessness thrown out, never to rot,
onto fly-tip at the edge of the wood.

I tried to ignore it, walking past every day.
What had it to do with me, this tatter
of ritual and custom, why should I feel sad
for it, sorry, as though it had a heart?

Someone propped it up. It shone like a star
from its position among the cypress's
graffiti and cruelly gouged out bark.

Birch, beech and oak relinquished their riches.
Larch took off her foxy gloves finger by finger.
Soon holly, ivy and redwoods only were green.
December's sepia muddied by rain
sank to deep browns even frost could not jewel.

Yet the tree shone, and all over Christmas
could be seen by children, at the edge of the wood,
shining. Only the snow could put it out.

Susan Richardson

NEREID

1.
The feeling caught me by surprise –
a sickle fin seeking to breach my spine
and the notion that sea-nymphing no longer satisfied.
Then   *click*   I found my new form by sound –
for a moment   *click click*   I was both dolphin and rider
then wholly *clickclickclick* the creature whose back
I'd sat astride.

                  Pleasure pods!
                           Bottlenosed joy!

I felt me vibrate with such echo-elation
that only the threat of nylon nets
              could unself me.

2.
When the urge returned, she yearned
    for land – to pugmark mud, stalk

on all fours, roar as her fur performed
    its striping. Yet each time she tigers now,

it's more tiring than before, as she hunts
    not just for prey but for pungent signs

that her kind has stopped declining.

3.
Next – ditch
backbone. Chill
blood. Don't
just itch
     to switch
to a glamour-mammal.
Meet Thetis the Remix –
inveterate invertebrate.
Stag beetle rootling
for putrid fruit
and sap, all set
to raise
     its mandibles
and fight
       for what remains
  of its habitat.

4.
Now roots shoot from soles; your torso's rigid. Leaves unfurl
from each twigit.
     You do little but   breathe   breathe   breathe,
then lead a meditation on the miracle of medicine in trees.
You'd shapestay in this way for growth-rings galore,
if it wasn't that your forest floor quakes
with that felling
              feeling.

5.
These days, when I crave to change, there are fewer forms to
choose from. Gone is the time when I could think 'corncrake'
and a reflex *crex* would swell my throat, when I could come over
all iguana and sense my neck blue-cresting. And as my skull
births twin horns and I bulge to megafauna, I can't decide if I'm
the last in the line. Or the Western Black Rhino in the savannah
of the mind.

Jocelyn Simms

MARKET DAY

John Scott rubs square palms across apron stripes.
I finger a sold apple.

Together we regard the sky: sulphureous clouds, nacreous
sun, the moon a cinnamon curl. *The Resurrection,*
Apocalypse, Turner's Fighting Téméraire?

I bite tart flesh, silver juices flow, the taste of almond
at the core. *Removal of any item of school uniform*
will result in nuclear fission.

What have we to lose, John Scott? Here, at the end
of the world ...

And you with all these pheasants to sell.

Jay Ramsay

HOT TUB

For Graham Meltzer

Beside the bowels of the University Hall
oaken, round beside a gallery of small steps
to hang your towel on: clothes left behind
and in the late evening light, clouded moon
beside pine trees, naked is spectral and soft
undefended, present in a man or woman
just being themselves: no strut, no ego
cloud-moon blended. My body said *go*
only my mind unsure of leaving its clothes
my body warmed through, and by chance conversation
with two strangers as familiar as anyone, human.
Nothing left to prove. Only that we love
its heat rising off your skin, its steam
breathing into the night air when it is enough
to be satisfied like this … as a hedgehog crosses your path;
and a gaggle of gathering geese call beyond
the last cars left on the road.

Desmond Kon Zhicheng-Mingdé

AFTER EMPHYSEMA

I.

It was a collective voice
we demanded of ourselves.

Something resonant, that echoed
against the cave walls.

We made a den of our bedrooms,
all four of them dimly lit.

We brought in fans, and tiled
our walls with brick and crepe.

Plato's Cave networked
like sea caves, so we always knew.

What each of us was thinking
or feeling, each an evensong.

"Eventually, the ravine is never deep
or surreal enough," Donovan said.

Or we were standing too far
from the outcrop or ridge.

Or we had shouted over each other,
adopting all the wrong angles.

II.

Or the wind was selfish, just carried
our voices, far away from us.

The romantic swirl of last year
no longer heady.

These days seem more daunting,
with your impending arrival.

The past remained like an afterthought,
even in its embellishments.

It remained
like some astrological forewarning.

Aloof, against a star
and its movement across a constellation.

About how today will bring about
a decision of dilemmas.

About tomorrow being more forgiving
and chancy, more efforted.

About us accommodating ourselves
to every whim of fate.

III.

About the month to come,
and how I should think about love.

And buying a lung,
and sticking to the plan.

And giving something back
as if life were a series of gifted moments.

Do I know what my father thinks of himself
or a child's death, even if it was so long ago?

Does memory have the same resilience
as history?

Does a love letter have the same transparency
as the memory it echoes?

What is the measure of my empathy?
There is not the intrusion in the small things.

The noticing glance or irreverent stare.
Nor is there the tedious recollection.

"There must be a lobe of a lung somewhere,"
Evan said, leaning in on Donovan.

IV.

Of an empty playground,
the living room looking unoccupied.

Its airless space recognizable
in every room these days.

The lounge in the library,
the corridor with its doorless thresholds.

The row of pews in the hilltop chapel,
the dug-out cave.

Its right side facing the setting sun,
the sun a shiver of light.

We pulled our leftovers out
from Evan's rucksack.

Four egg tarts squashed into one corner,
pastry collapsed into the custard.

Like a bread pudding.
My hand pried open one side of the box.

Soggy cardboard, as the rest of the box
caved in like a house.

Mark Totterdell

DAMSON

Another autumn,
and I'm on the same ladder,
up the same old tree, in the garden
of the house where I was born.

These roots run deep, though gales
have ripped off limbs. Between the clouds
my radio briefly comes to life;
'...*thousands...across the border...*'

Each fruit needs tearing from its stalk.
Their bloom rubs off. They darken.
It's only later that I see the light.
The journey of a word. Damascene.

Clare Whistler

ACROSS LINES

I was dreaming about trees
four trees that became fish
turning back and forth
twitching and gobbling
hats tight over fish faces

in the outskirts of the dream
tractors, generators and men
were doing the work of the wood
judges and totems
four in a row like trees

working, cutting, hoisting,
skinning, stacking trees
on the other side of the wall
the four crossed the line
between woods and men

I knew it was about trees
and the fight for trees
and the woman, arriving
at her future, dressed
sap-blooded, as the man

John Freeman

THE POND IN THE FIELDS

Which was the moment that seemed an answer
to that intense passage of meditation,
insight into familiar thoughts that gave
a quality of second sight, amplified,
like rising milk in a pan that overflows,
or the moment a singer moves and echo
starts to redouble what she has been singing?

Was it when I turned on to that foot-path?
As soon as I did the day came to life.
Grassy banks enclosing trodden earth made it
a little Eden, overhung with trees.
I came to a stile at a pylon's foot
and climbed into a field, and all this seemed
new, though it was only renewed, including
views back over the brow of the green slope.
And on the other side of me, westwards,
a lonely pond I'd forgotten existed,
nestling in the hollow of the fields, glistened,
mirroring bright sky, so sky and water
seemed not to know which was which, any more
than the tangled branches of a fallen tree
knew which part of them was just reflected
and which was solid wood rising from water,
though agitated ripples wondered whether
breeze or some unseen life was shaking them.

That was the top of the walk, and just then
I saw a wren start from a hedge near me,
and after treading round hardened mud, gaining
the lane with no harm to town shoes, I saw
on the verge in gloom this year's first primroses.
So I'll take that as the moment that answered –
that vision of the gleaming pond between grass
and sky, black branches rising out of it –
that answered my visionary confluence
of familiar thoughts, that Edward Thomas
had died young and been lamented over
as part of that great wave of tragedy
that engulfed Europe a century ago
and yet had lived on, especially today,
March the third, in the hearts of his readers,
and our minds, our walking bodies, our eyes,
seeing the world with vision he had sharpened –
and then it was he showed me the dew pond
or, as it seemed, touching me for an instant
with his spirit, saw it through my eyes.

Simon Williams

TROPIC CASCADE
after George Monbiot

If you take a dozen wolves
from Saskatchewan or Manitoba,
release them slowly into Yellowstone,

If they eat elk and bison (a few)
start them moving from the
plains to the sides of valleys,

If the grass and trees recover;
aspen, pine and cottonwood,
grow taller, thicker, lay down roots,

If their cover gives chance to
field mice and songbirds, hence
badgers, foxes and coyotes,

If the grasslands recover
and the trees cling on to soil
that might have washed away,

If the river banks are stabilised
and beavers make more pools
for otters, ducks and muskrats,

that's how wolves change
the course of rivers. Call it out
across the whole caldera.

Alison Hill

PENDULUM

The energy of a swing still in motion
when the sirens wails, calling their own.
Echoes of their laughter still dangling
on a drift of breeze, leaves swirling.

Later, we hope, those children taste only
the moment, the casual drip of honey,
alive to the here and the now –
chances they will find along the way.

Tunde Oseni

WE ARE ALL RED INSIDE

One sunny Sunday
I ran across the Park
And I jogged along the mark
As I looked left and right
I saw faces around the pitch
Kindred of Mother Nature within reach
Wandering about
In the sea of life
From wherever each of us may come
And whichever race each of us may claim
Only one race indeed exists
And that is the human race
White, black, blue or brown
'We are all red inside'

Wendy Sloan

DEAD YOUNG THING

"Leave it out back" he said, "No one will know".
And no one did. And no one cared or thought
about us. Why would they? I went to school
like everybody else. I looked the same –
a little quieter. Yeah, I was scared,
mostly at night. The daytime was all right

until I started feeling sick again.
I prayed the faint would go away. It did.
But I kept getting bigger and I hid
myself in looser clothes. He never stopped,
before or after. Anyway, I knew
he never would. I left it, like he said,
inside the dumpster by the courtyard stair.
Then we would go on like we had before,
but this one cried, and lived, and we got caught.

I still can't sleep at night. I have this dream:
he picks me up, I'm screaming as I fall
down on the garbage slime. You see, it's me
was dead for him, right from the start. Since I'm
in jail, I've got a better place to be.

Margie Gaffron

CABIN FEVER

For so long, living cocooned in your head
imagined conversations repeat
words needing voice,
snowed in,
frozen tight, nothing
can get loose
even within the four walls of a warm house
with the people you live with, you love
comes a time when you are ready
to tell the first stranger you meet
your whole life's story
and the words, once they begin their welling
don't stop, can't stop,
they flow like spring swelling streams
from a distance you can see
but no more slow it than you can slow
the ache, come March
the right time and one warm day
to take off the insular layers
grown tough about the self like calluses
to be immersed in the new season
to claim it for your own, wrapped about you
and then to cast off even this newly forming skin
and leave it, smoldering
in some open doorway behind you.

Chris O'Carroll

HABITAT

In an expanse of reeds, two blackbirds nest.
One wears on either wing a scarlet patch;
One sports gold plumage on its head and breast.
Their voices, like those markings, do not match,
The yellow-head's unmusical and harsh.
When both birds seek the nesting sites they need,
Their competition subdivides the marsh:
The red-wing, marginally the smaller breed,
Must make do at the margins, while its rival
Conquers the choicer center to hold sway
Where slightly deeper water aids survival
By keeping land-based predators at bay.
   Via such nuance is one habitat
   Parsed into this distinctive realm and that.

Andie Lewenstein

EARTH AND STARS

It's workshop night upstairs in the Earth and Stars.
Strip everything away, says the poet,
See what's there.

We shift on wooden chairs and try to penetrate
the plastered brickwork walls for some illuminating
or discreet epiphany.

The moon-faced girl with golden eyes says
What if there's nothing, like opening the cupboard,
finding it bare?

That's poetry, he says and rubs his hands
what more do you want? Earth and stars and
nothing in between but this.

We share the thin light of a forty watt bulb and stare at the
candle stuck to a cracked white saucer
on which everything depends.

Downstairs it's time. Women in black boots wipe tables,
sweep the boards, stack metal ashtrays - jukebox croons
Are the Stars Out Tonight?

And moonface slips away into the clear and empty street.
Skipping over pavement cracks, her eyes reflect the light
of streetlamps. She sings as she goes home.

Mark Haworth-Booth

WATER SONNET

Watching a pond - or not looking at it,
then glancing down - I notice on the water
flat pewter: an oval set in shifting silver.
The breeze must make this patch of water matte
or maybe someone polishing the pond
just kissed it with a waxed-up duster leaving
a smear to even-out in widening
circles across the rest. See how it's pinned
there by the wind, keeping its form, this phantom,
like breath misting the surface of a mirror.
I keep company with my chimera
until it shapes away, going and gone,
its geometry dissolving in cats paws
as the rain arrives with a patter of applause.

Sarah Beckett & Martha Landman

PLAY SCARLATTI WHILE YOU PACK: A DUET

"Make an inventory", he said. Restless,
you pace from room to room
barefoot on cool tiles.

Small treasured things don't weigh much:
blue vase, a heart-shaped stone
ceramic angel hanging over the door.

Lemon light
floods the empty studio. Two easels
work stool, trestle tables

all packed away
heart stripped like the house
down to the bone.

The windows get bigger. You wonder
if you could weigh the blue whoo-whoo
of the wood dove at evening

measure the sound of rain on the galvanize
guess the cubic footage of yellow trumpet flowers
lolling on their vines.

He says, "Your tiger days striped blue and gold
won't fit in the container. "

　　　　I make my list and find
　　　　the places I've been
　　　　and the mountains I've seen,
　　　　the stars at night
　　　　in Lagos and Trinidad, in Sicily

and in Spain
all hold the same truth —

My life in a box, suitcase in hand
I find the sun in every city

I keep moving for a different view
Somewhere the soil is black, elsewhere
rivers open into the ocean

When at last I turn my face to the rain
I have nowhere to call home

It is said you can find the sun
in every city but no one
mentions London.

Soon you will leave a Calypso life
luggage full of goodbyes
'Sweet, Sweet Trinidad' ringing in your ears.

The sea takes no notice.
Unaware of your arrival
it ignores your leaving

too busy with its sea-ness
to bother with a small presence
up on the cliff

waterfalls of cloud plunging
over the horizon, tom-tom heart
beating in time with the sea.

When the curlews keep me awake
on quiet nights

and the bushfires smell hot
memories of places linger
between leaving and arriving

Swallows and red-footed falcons
fly from Europe
buffaloes migrate
under the wild Africa sun
and mind maps travel
across canyons and woods and caves

At the call for a southbound train
I change my letterbox

Play Scarlatti while you pack
or Miles — any music
that's blue and gold.

Cover the sofa draped in dawn, birdsong
and the wine-dark trees. Bubble-wrap
your tiger days. Seal up the moon.

In the evening
tuck the sun into a pocket
one last time before heading North

your shadow stretched behind
in dazzly light, raindrops bouncing
on the roof.

You begin to imagine warmth indoors
instead of out, the slap
of cold air on your face

a robin singing.

Anne Stewart

FOR A CHANGE

something innocent this way comes.

No learned cynicism, no imminent threat.

See it as some long-haired girl not tanned yet
looking to do some good in the world.

Maybe she wants to be a paramedic.
Bike it in fast to where only a bike can get.

She wants to save a body at least
if not a soul.

Let it be catching. Let it come to us all
like an infection.

Let it be this Local
this Determined
Unstoppable

as the saints and angels
of our every day.

We are the cells it needs
to go viral.

Caroline Gill

WEDDELL SEAL AT THE ICE EDGE

Winds slice through McMurdo Sound,
        ruffling wrinkles on a young seal.
She raises a flipper
to receive a tickle, before
        her departure to a surreal
underwater realm
of snow-globe chill and starless ocean.

Who knows or charts the colour
        of this bubble, bounded by walls
that float? The juvenile
swims to maturity, passing
        echo chambers and empty halls.
Icebergs define these
shadowlands of forgotten silence.

What will happen when the seal
        surfaces? She may find a gale
howling as snow-drifts melt,
turning polar mountains to slush.
        Could an opportunistic whale
breach a dangling world
or shake a globule to smithereens?

Winds slice through McMurdo Sound:
        and in their wake a creature flaps
the spray with flippered side.
Glass droplets burst: the seal plunges
        through coral spheres, as water wraps
around her. She holds
her breath, cocooned for sixty minutes.

Andie Lewenstein

DUNBEATH

Here it is enough to discover
a piece of mica on the beach,

see how it turns in the sun
to silver. As a child, you had the power

to transform everything. Broken glass
was precious cargo. Wise as the fool

who traded gold for withered apples,
you knew the names of things.

Now it is enough to see a small brown
bird on a wet stone,

its leg as thin as wheat grass,
looking at you.

A single note half-taken by the wind
but your ear catches it. Is this the sign

that you have come so far to find
in the mid-day light –

thin strand of bird call,
watchful eye?

Kay Green

RED FLASH

Although moments aren't distinct in a solitary sun-soaked stroll
I now delineate a hedgerow moment in order to create
a memory.

Sunday afternoon. Me standing
on grass between woods and ditch.
Clouds of meadowsweet quivering
although I don't remember a breeze
just heat. Before my chosen moment
the meadowsweet had been whispering
a hot reflection on the cooler clouds above.
I was there, and had been there. Also the flowers.
Me breathing, watching, sweating.
The good ache in my hot legs
as I bent to touch the fragrant aspirin drifts…

CHROME LOOM RED METAL COME
HOT BLACK PLASTIC AND NOISE gone

That was the moment
and it strikes me
that when I'm driving
I often wonder why
the lonely people I pass
are standing in nowhere
between town and town
on the side of the road
with no life

… when the dullness of petrol
is diffused in the sun
I know the car is gone, and
the foaming blooms nod
and life swells the air around me
and Sunday accepts me back
and the fuzzy meadowsweet quivers
near the hot tarmac strip
that was put there for a purpose
after all.

Susan Taylor

THEATRE OF NOW

Only let one finger meet another,
register the touch, though light,
creates an almost-dimple on the skin
and urges the shared condition of life.

There's not a pen or brushstroke
rises to this contact,
though done in stunning hues
like the presence of a rose,

or scraped with something dancing
like a lobster's claw on sand
that's flattened by heavies
rolling in the tide.

Tall grasses, which grow up around us,
share with us these fluid walls.
Everywhere, we mow greenesses down;
walk on carpets, clipped and groomed:

our feet, familiar
with hard killed pods of skin,
our heads with the pressure
of polished words.

Only let my fingers meet another's,
feel the present pulling through;
by some miracle,
our bodies have permeable walls.

Camilla Lambert

CURLY LEAVES ALL DANCE AS THE WIND BLOWS

There have been songs since morning, Gaudeamus,
Leaves dancing circles round the moon, Ferryman
carry me home, and Gaudeamus again; voices
bursting from grey to shades of vermillion, scarlet,
closer, farther, blending and unwinding like plaits
of hair tumbling down Rapunzel's tower, twisting
round the room, glancing off the windows, sliding
over oak banisters to the flagged kitchen where
someone has left the door open, and on the floor
curly leaves dance as the wind rises up, letting
the outside in, undeniable, like thunder, like time,
undeniable like Gaudeamus, and the ferry man
rowing from shore to shore and the spangled leaves
of the birch trees fletching to the moon and back.

Margaret Wilmot

THE OX-SKIN BAG

The train soon to arrive and you look up
from a book, still in another world, and see
another world, not known the way the slope and slant
of the fields near home is known beyond awareness.
Here the angles are sharp, the light falls
obliquely, almost black within deep folds.

Maybe while you've been reading
the train has taken a different fork, you're being borne
at great speed away from the place where
you are so eager to arrive.

Like Odysseus asleep: how in sight
of Ithaca his crew untie the ox-skin bag of winds.
Now they will have to face cannibals, metamorphoses,
unpredictable magic; the underworld itself –
and only Odysseus will return.

Maxine Backus

A GOOD DEATH

We kept our own vigil. Not at the hospital.
We propitiated the spirits of the hearth.

First we took tea and toast and gossiped gently.
His mother in her fiery red kimono. She talked of

good deaths she had known, had known a few,
being a nurse. I remembered riding pillion with him

on the bikers' outing to Eyam. Suddenly we
whined with grief: he was slated for today,

his dance of death over. Lunch, white wine,
to fortify us for the journey, a ceremony.

We grew quite merry, raising our glasses
to cheer him on his way. When the phone call

came we were ready to leave. I was merely the driver:
she would see him through his final rite of passage.

Jean-Mark Sens

SATELLITES

Satellites can fall anywhere, but unlikely it will be you.
           Times Picayune, September 21 2011

Naively when a child you may have believed the moon
      could fall
lose its suspension an invisible breath held up like a balloon
      full of helium.
You never questioned its disappearance
only its hugeness growing from a thumb mark behind clouds
till obstructing the horizon at the end of Calle San Pedro
a paper lantern with its glow you pulled down closer
the kitchen table where you copied series of little masts
      "t" letters
invisible hulls running the lines, the fading of a tugboat.
A parliament of nuns assembled in the school yard
you saw once you came early to play the piano with
      your mother
wondering from where in the night they had stepped
      into their habits.
Sora Lucia at recess you surprisingly tugged at her hand
as if to check her limbs were real like yours.
You only found the answer of her cold wet hand, a slim smile.
The bell each pull on the clapper you could descry to the
      last tremors on its lip
all to return to the square white solitude of note books—
a fear tangible, taut , a rope as a ship snaps its moorings
wharf and hull parting to a widening length of sea.
Of fears there were of course the cold war, nuclear drills
you still like to retell today.
Sora Lucia gone a day after you tugged at her
had you shaken something under her garb?
A nun's secret, small bone of faith inside her rigid neck?

You learned that year the afterlife of nerves dissecting frogs.
You must have moved to another port city,
the nuns merely became a back drop of undifferentiated women
with their moments of a distant election,
as you today you read on the front page—satellites can fall
anywhere—unlikely, will it be you—Sora Lucia, your tugging
    at her,
what falls—probabilities or predestination.

Irena Pasvinter

I AM A SHIP

I am a ship. I used to brave the storms,
Enjoyed the challenge of seafaring gods,
But nowadays I nourish hungry worms –
They feast beneath my skin; my body rots.

Time was, my sails relished howling winds
And flew me like an arrow through wild blasts.
Too bad today they hang, my broken wings,
Pierced by protruding bones of naked masts.

I'm still not done. Waves carry me, I strive,
But on my way through endless ports and docks
I ponder breaking free from wretched life
By smashing on inviting deadly rocks.

And yet there are souls that love me even now –
Love anchors me, denies my final bow.

Alison Lock

KANDAHAR

A boy finds a fallen star

from a pocket of treasures
his hand reaches out

pulls the loop that is trip-wired
to a hurricane, it lifts him high

higher to a crescent of incandescence
then down he flitters in a shower

of pomegranate seeds seeping the ground
sweet red, dark red, black red.

Now there is light, swinging bright
he waves back with a bound stub

as if reaching for a moonbeam.

Christina Lloyd

POSTCARDS

Darwin, Australia

You told me how the crocs were baited
from the river's mud milk, how jagged smiles
surfaced for the show; a hunk of meat swinging
from a stick was all the tour guide's taunt entailed.

You marveled at the foolish rush to the railings to watch
the beasts leap and snap. The boat tipped to one side—
you stayed put starboard, a self-appointed steward.

San José, Costa Rica

In the serpentarium, sheepish amidst the glass terraria
we scanned labels for genus, species, habitat, quick to shirk
the fer-de-lance, its green skin and helixed muscle.

We ventured through, sidewinding toward the exit
to escape a gloved keeper geared up to milk for venom.

Brisbane, Australia

A water dragon joins me by a hotel swimming pool. It basks
freely, my presence protection from the butcher-birds.
Guessing by the newness of its claws, a yearling.

It left the soft soil of its mother's chamber, idling at her burrow
to then wander the suburbs. We take each other in,
understanding
our place in these parts. Our covenant, to leave each other be.

San Francisco, California

Father, I take in the life of my six-week-old embryo
through a pink medical drawing: eye spot, arm bud, tail.

The heart bulge fills with our blood; hands and feet
form slowly, paddling in the dark.

Amarjit Chandan

GRAMMAR OF BEING

God uttered a word: *Kun** Be – and it was.
Be is the seed of all verbs.
So many verbs make a noun.
The noun is the fruit
      the seed ripened waiting to be sown again.
It's the end of the continuous verb
      happening in the present perfect
            all the time.
The noun is the ultimate verb
      of conception   of bearing that reaches its
end
        of no end.
The pyramid rests on the triangled tense.
The noun is the point on the pyramid top
      where the journey starts towards the timeless
        in the present.

* *Arabic word*

John McCullough

SLEEPING HERMAPHRODITE

Asleep? I'm watching you through my lids.
This isn't easy, tracking your nebulous shape
while you assess my neck's turn, slide
down to smooth cleavage, tummy, waist

then encounter what's stashed below my thigh.
Here I am, unveiled as arguable,
a mishmash of harbour and ship – the stay
in thought when all ideas are possible.

I'm everything yet deeply ill-equipped
for solitude. What I need to know
is whether you ache to prise free

the ankle I've left loosely wrapped
in a sheet. Singlespeak is boring. Let's talk toes
and honey. Come on, nosey boy. Surprise me.

Richard J.N. Copeland

A KIND OF BLUE

Cool, the colour of iceberg
or a sun warmed sky,
the shade of feeling
a mood transmuted.

He waits for the bass riff,
a nine note opening, horn poised,
blows just two.
No one knows what comes next

or how it will flow
with cymbal swish opening
free thought expression
held with downcast eyes

reaching the ear
the colour of sound
not raced but walked
to a beat that turns

the mind's wheel
sent to its limit
a muted voice;
a new kind of blue.

Pansy Maurer-Alvarez

NIGHTFALL

Oh wondrous night, where is your prow?

Interior images
seem to escape from a cave near water level
although I thought
I saw lunar landscapes a minute ago

Receding voices line the walls like shadowy figurines
Warm draught
stir a faint scent
Jutting rock shapes look like actors in metallic light

A requiem of rain
murmurs above the breaking of the waves
Is that tragedy in my singing voice? Will there be
tragedy along this voyage?

Our imaginary forces are so emotionally charged;
what it means to have once been
a child comes back,
the life side and the death side

Loneliness
because the child's hand in the parent's
is an outline barely visible in this portion of night

Jackie Wills

LETTER

Her letter's disturbing the sorting office,
its mortgage applications, insurance forms.

Brown ink on a thick cream envelope.
Is there a hand squashed inside, a pelt?

The postman feels it move in his bag, restless,
but it calms as he meanders the streets,

walked back to sleep so an older script,
fainter, can appear on paper turned to vellum,

tracing four ponies emerging from woods.
So much she has yet to tell him.

Lennart Lundh

PLUS TARDE, LES LANGUES DES AMATEURS

Later, as the sunset fades on the living room wall,
they sit in cold blue lightning
and the warmth of the fire they've started.
In accents reserved for foreign things
they speak of childhood sounds,
the smell of sewing machines
and Friday bars at closing time,
the aftertaste of murdered love.

Later, after the curtains turn down the street light,
they write essays in tongues across foreign lands.
They read each other in the Braille of lovers.
They search maps on which there are no monsters.
The fire burns long, but not forever.
They sleep, pages in a book
nestled beneath the covers,
as the ink dries on the chapter.

Later, as the sunrise makes its way across them,
they sit almost naked at the kitchen table,
sift the ashes with silences as well as words,
find the embers whispering of kindle and flame
hot enough to weld two tightly, given laters.
Later, they will lose the vocabularies of the past,
burning letters cast in scripts they no longer recognize,
or need to remember against the silent night.

William Ayot

BETWEEN THE MOUNTAINS
For a friend, leaving on a quest

Dear friend, forget the wisdom of words –
the truth out there lies in wood, stone and water.
Leave your maps and judgments in your pack,
so you get closer to the language of things.
That way you can let your body do the listening.

Don't get too excited by operatic sunsets:
their blowsy, look-at-me, grabs for attention
are all very well — and beautiful enough —
but their gaudy colours and theatrical declines
won't teach you much you couldn't learn at home.

Whenever possible, try to greet the dawn —
between first light and sunrise comes a ritual,
where the quiet waiting, and the stretching of time,
the cold, and the boredom, and the dawning of humility,
sow the seeds of a faith, or the deepest belonging.

If you can, just once, stand naked under the sky.
Let the moon and the sun see who you really are.
The stars will not shame you, nor the wind;
the aspens and junipers will offer silent blessing,
while the giving earth will guide you on your way.

For everything, like you, is journeying to something:
the rocks and the ravens, the grasses and the pines;
flowering and fruiting, falling and crumbling,
trembling and dancing in the sunlit valley
that lies between the mountains of birth and death.

Susan Skinner

A WIND IS IN THE ROSE
From Paul Klee's painting Rose Wind

Even in our land of birth
a wind is in the rose,
trespassing
the dark red centre.

a wind is in the rose,
in the circle of petals,
the dark red centre.
Rose wind you are invisible

in the circle of petals
that float above the earthen pot.
Rose wind you are invisible!
Streaks of light

that float above the earthen pot
track your unseen weather,
streaks of light
drive the roses's colour,

track your unseen weather.
Wind, you have absorbed the rose,
driven the rose's colour
into winter ice.

You have absorbed the rose
into the universe,
into winter ice,
upward into the final stars.

Jeff Cloves

GARDENS OF EARTHLY DELIGHT

never mind mountain ranges
vast deserts steppes prairies
veldt tundra ice-cap
lakes rivers stupendous falls
and all
the other wonders
of the known world
turn your mind instead
to gardens –
back gardens that is
not the estates of the mighty –
to those most intimate
private territories of the soul
tended loved largely unmapped
no matter what continent
what climate
what skin
each one a landmark
in somebody's life
the gardeners of the world
united in their love
of a bit of ground
to call their own
their source of hope
expectation
fulfilment
disappointment
solace wonder
retreat and meditation
I'm planting myself in the garden
believe me
between the potatoes and parsley

*believe me**
sang a friend
who knew what he was about
and spoke for the multitude
who know for sure –
should they acknowledge their hearts –
that if we planted and tilled
instead of poisoned and killed
everything in the garden
would be lovely
believe me

*from Bill Fay's 'Garden Song'

Marc Harshman

WHAT THERE IS

A slow, sifting snow,
and here and there
a patch of earth glows with it.
Just enough of a tear in the sky,
enough of a slit
to let the sun work its light
upon the fragile frost--
a million downy crystals
ignite,
and you would almost think,
you just might,
that there was a path out there
where the cold is gathering.

Beth Somerford

PUTTING THE GARDEN TO BED

Somewhere between
the first leaf's and the last fruit's-fall,
sometime around harvest,
with dying campanula
and a bonfire's fusty incense,
she makes her inter-solstice ritual
with measured calm
and not a little resignation.
The garden wayward, overgrown,
is no protestant-hard landscape,
and has a certain pavèd craziness.
She has burned the heretic horsetail,
grounded adolescent brambles,
and now demands a quiet order.
It is late in the day and not a time
to get ones-selves excited.
I watch her as she tuckles in
the clipped and quilted edges,
sweeps the crumbs and debris
from the grassy counterpane;
absent-minded, cossets up
the tender figs in gossamer,
flicks the strands of overgrowth
and mutters her goodnights.

Simon Zonenblick

JUNIPER

I want to see Juniper.

Not driveways or dual carriageways
but Juniper,
to open the door to its green greeting,
just a single stem, one tree
to guard against the plague.

I am open to all species -
Chinese, common, the cedarish lace columns
of softwooded *Juniperus virginiana*,
pencil cedar, whose long-needled juvenility
bears lime-like ovals of dehiscent green,
aromatic, heartwood of rose-red, inward bleeding,
sistering Hibernica, communis of the purpling fruits, savin,
hybrids with their bluish berries ripening roundly like the
glimmering gems of delicate necklaces.

And if I cannot see it, I'll imagine Juniper.
My thoughts and angers, my anxieties,
those last thoughts
passing through the brain as I drift to sleep
like the revs of cars half-heard deep in the night,
all will be sharpened in the shape of Junipers,
their stoicism, spindling twigs and petioles,
their daggered leaves, love-bladed,
hanging like manicured fingers.

I will imagine Juniper,
dream their gin-sting and their brown dye gifts,
their ancient acid foliage, their voluptuous,
medicinal fruits

Just as I imagine you,
perennial and spicily defensive, hardy
but becoming more elusive

Linda Black

SAYS THE ONLOOKER:

I see you are painting

And so she is, with brushes, various in breadth and temperament, dripped in mud. (To proceed she needed to know.)

It began, says she, without form – base and mired, a little relentless (she used to etch with the point of a needle) took me by surprise. I didn't question, didn't despair – difficult to sustain an interest I carried on, applied thick strokes, began to see I could begin again: from clod and clump and barren consternation a tree could be, brushed into leaf, to vein; twig corresponding to lacewing, linnet, leitmotif.

Something removed; something arising

From over her shoulder he diverts her endeavours. At first her world is murky, a grimy realm, flat and cracked, conspiring to obfuscate. She doesn't mind such meddlesome ways: when he says *you need only look up,* she does from her engrossment. (It seems he is wiser than she.) Such a downpour! A fountain of colour! Where once was marsh and quicksand, a firebird flies, dips its wings in sunset, circles, calls to another.

How will you know when it's finished?

Roselle Angwin

MIDWINTER SOLSTICE

Just now, in the full night of midwinter's night
over the traffic and the cop-cars and the late shoppers,
down at the bottom of the hill in the car park
where the red dogwoods flame, a robin started up
her strong ribbon of song in the lee of the storm, and as I
drive up the hill, window open to let in the dark,
a second tunes in, and then on the brow another,
each singing its loud hymn to the night and the cloud
and the brimming tapers of stars between, and this,
this, must surely be grace, a moment's inbreath, in our
onwards rush, on this northern side of this lost-in-space
spinning-back-towards-the-light planet, our home star.

Rose Flint

PRAYER FOR ALWAYS PEACE

I ask all the animals to open their mouths
to howl this prayer for peace

I ask all the birds to lift their songs to the winds
and sing this prayer for peace

I ask all the trees and flowers, all that is green growing
to open their hollow throats where the sap runs
to call this prayer for peace

I ask the rocks to dream this prayer for peace

I ask the sand to rearrange its grains
and write this prayer for peace

I ask the ocean wave to shout this prayer for peace
or whisper it on the lonely listening beaches
where the rivers will send it upstream
in the willing breath of fish

I ask the deep wells to give rise to this prayer for peace

I ask the holy hills to toll this prayer for peace

I ask the stars to shine the spelling
of this prayer for peace

and the moon and the sun pause in the sky
as night and day, as right and left, as east and west
as all that is opposite yet may still come into balance
in harmony with this world, and in time

I ask for every candleflame to ignite this prayer for peace
so that this prayer is in the world and of the world
and becomes the world and the world is peace.

Michaela Ridgway

UP

past jammed-together houses
doors all shut, faces lit

by TV screens, past a boy
racing down the street

— a woman's voice
falling faster still behind him

the trick is to keep a steady pace
past lampposts

a clutch of honeysuckle buds
the pub with no name

a rope-swing
slung from the dying elm

and past mum, with daisies in her hair
and dad, cross-legged on a mountain-top

past the scent of mangoes as they ripen
in the dark, and up

past the time when my heart almost stopped.
Don't dilly-dally. Lengthen your stride

note the flock of geese as they rise
from the lake and fly up

past a choir of trees with branches raised
their leaves falling, upwards

and up, to the line that marks the top of the hill
the sudden sheer sky

Michaela Ridgway

THIS MORNING I BRING YOU TOMATOES

Crystals in the window spin rainbows
across your living room floor.

This morning I bring you tomatoes
and old Spanish proverbs.

As I read aloud, you fold each word,
cast a staircase

of them into the cut-glass cosmos,
and at last bid me climb.

Meet the Contributors

Patricia Ace's pamphlet *First Blood* was published by HappenStance Press in 2006. Her first full collection, *Fabulous Beast*, was published by Freight Books in March 2013. She has been placed and won prizes in many national poetry competitions. Her poem 'Papa Joe' won the Plough Poetry Prize in 2010 and 'Saying goodbye to my daughter at night' was selected for the online anthology *20 Best Scottish Poems 2013*. Since 2013 she has been collaborating with Edinburgh artist, Lindy Furby, to produce poetry postcards as part of *The Written Image* project. Her work is featured in *Be the First to Like This: New Scottish Poetry*, edited by Colin Waters and published in 2014.

Afam Akeh is Founder and Director of the Centre for African Poetry. His first book of poems, *Stolen Moments*, was published in 1988. He is also the author of *Letter Home and Biafran Nights* (2012). Akeh has won or been listed for awards in poetry, the short story and journalism. In his many years of editorial practice, he has interviewed leading African authors, also assisting publishers of African literature in curating and reviewing work by these authors. Founding Editor of *African Writing Online*, he has presented his work at international literary events, the BBC and various UK venues. *Ghosts,* his third collection of poems is expected in 2015.

Roselle Angwin is a poet and author based near Dartmoor. She leads workshops, courses and retreats in writing and ecopsychology in Southwest Britain, the Hebrides, and France. www.fire-in-the-head.co.uk www.thewildways.co.uk

William Ayot is a poet, author, ritualist, and teacher. His three collections of poetry include *E-mail from the Soul,* (PS Avalon) which won the People's Book Prize. He currently runs "On the Border", a poetry series, in Chepstow and is poet-in-residence at Oxford University's Saïd Business School. www.williamayot.com

Catherine Ayres is a teacher, living and working in Northumberland. Her poems have appeared in Ink, Sweat & Tears, Spontaneity, Domestic Cherry, Prole and The Moth. She recently came third in Ambit magazine's "Under the Influence" competition. Her poetry often explores difference and how loss can separate a person from one world and lead them to another.

Nnorom Azuonye studied Dramatic Arts at the University of Nigeria, Nsukka and has worked as an actor, scene designer and theatre director. A Methodist Local Preacher, businessman and widely published writer, he founded the Sentinel Poetry Movement in 2002 and is the founding Chief Executive Officer and Publishing Director of SPM Publications – an imprint of Sentinel Writing & Publishing Company Limited. Author of *Letter to God & Other Poems, The Bridge Selection: Poems for the Road*, and *Funeral of the Minstrel* (a play), his poems, short stories, interviews and essays have appeared in *Opon Ifa, African Writing, Agenda, Orbis, DrumVoices Revue, Flair*, and *For the Love of God* among other publications. Website: www.nnoromazuonye.com

Maxine Backus is originally from Leicester, now living near Zurich. She studied Philosophy and Poetry in English (M. Phil., Stirling). She has worked mainly as a translator and interpreter in the banking industry, has run creative writing classes in England and Switzerland and taught poetry at university level. Maxine has self-published two collections of poetry in English, with German translations.

S.M.Beckett. Artist-Poet S.M Beckett has been writing poetry for several years and has participated in many public poetry readings. Her poetry has been featured in Maco Magazine, Wings of Desire Catalogue, Malaleuca and she was designated Poet of the Month in the December issue of *Caught in the Net,* the Poetry Kit's online site.

James Bell has published two poetry collections *the just vanished place (2008)* and *fishing for beginners (2010),* both from *tall-lighthouse.* Born in Scotland he now lives in Brittany where he contributes articles and photographs to an English language journal and continues to publish poems nationally and internationally with recent print appearances in: *The Journal, Elbow Room, Shearsman, Tears In The Fence, Under The Radar and Upstairs at Du Roc.*

Jim Bennett, has written 74 books and numerous chapbooks and pamphlets in a 48 year career as a poet. Jim lives near Liverpool in the UK and tours giving readings of his work throughout the year. He is widely published and has won many competitions and awards for poetry and performance. He runs one of the world's most successful internet sites for poets; www.poetrykit.org

Linda Black received the 2004/5 Poetry School Scholarship and won the 2006 New Writing Ventures Award for Poetry. *The beating of wings* (Hearing Eye, 2006) was the PBS Pamphlet Choice for Spring 2007, when she also received an Arts Council Writer's Award. Her collections are *Inventory* and *Root*, (Shearsman 2008 & 2011) and *The Son of a Shoemaker* (Hearing Eye 2012). The latter consists of collaged prose-poems, based on the early life of Hans Christian Andersen, plus the author's pen and ink illustrations. It was the subject of a Poetry Society exhibition in April 2013. She is co-editor of Long Poem Magazine www.longpoemmagazine.org.uk

Peter Branson lives in Rode Heath, East Cheshire. A former teacher and lecturer, Peter is well known in the region as a traditional-style singer, songwriter and poet. His poetry has been accepted for publication by many journals in Britain, the USA, Canada, Ireland, Australasia and South Africa. He has won and been placed in quite a few poetry competitions over recent years, including The Grace Dieu, The Petra Kenny, The Envoi and The Wigtown. His latest book, Red Hill, Selected Poems, 2000-2012, by Lapwing, Ireland, came out in May 2013.

Lesley Burt lives in Christchurch, Dorset. Her poetry has been published online and in magazines and anthologies including *Tears in the Fence*, *The Interpreters House*, *Sarasvati* and *The Cinnamon Anthology*. Her chapter, 'Considering connotation: the impact and implications of language in poetry' is included in *Teaching Creative Writing* (2012) ed. Elaine Walker. She is currently a student undertaking an MA in Creative Writing (Distance Learning) at Lancaster University.

David Caddy's most recent books include *The Bunny Poems* (Shearsman Books, 2011), *So Here We Are* (Shearsman Books, 2012) and *Cycling After Thomas And The English* (Spout Hill Books, 2013). He edits *Tears in the Fence* magazine, writes criticism, organises writing workshops, a poetry reading series, and directs an annual poetry festival.

Judith Cair was born in Somerset. She has worked as a potter in rural potteries and as a teacher in an urban middle school. In 2013 a pamphlet of her poetry, *The Ship's Eye*, was published by Pighog Press. She has also written articles for *Artemis* on modern interpretations of classical texts.

R. T. Calway is Anglo-Welsh and has worked much of her life outdoors, but found time for an Open University degree and a Master's at Cardiff University. For ten years she ran her own arboriculture business. A selection of her prose and verse was published in the anthology Black Waves in Cardiff Bay (Cinnamon, 2008). She has been short-listed for several literary prizes including the Impress Prize in 2012.

Michael Cantor's full-length collection, *Life in the Second Circle* (Able Muse Press, 2012), was a finalist for the 2013 Massachusetts Book Award for Poetry. A chapbook, *The Performer*, was published in 2007. His work has appeared in *The Dark Horse, Measure, Raintown Review, SCR, Chimaera, The Flea*, and numerous other journals and anthologies. A native New Yorker, he has lived and worked in Japan, Latin America and Europe, and presently divides his time between Plum Island, MA, and Santa Fe, NM.

Amarjit Chandan has published seven collections of poetry and three books of essays in Punjabi and two in English *Sonata for Four Hands* prefaced by John Berger (Arc, 2010). His work has appeared in many anthologies including in the periodicals including in Arabic, Brazilian-Portuguese, Greek, Italian, Romanian and Turkish. He was amongst British poets on Radio 4 selected by Andrew Motion on National Poetry Day in 2001. He has participated in the Aldeburgh, Ledbury, King's Lynn and Winchester and Didim Poetry Festivals held in the UK and Turkey respectively.

Helen Clare. In a previous life Helen Clare was a science teacher - she now works on projects which combine science poetry and learning, including a poetry residency at the Museum of Science and Industry in Manchester. Her published work includes Mollusc (Comma, 2004) and Entomology (Happenstance 2014) and her poems have won a number of national prizes, including First Prize in the London Writers

Competition 2002, and Runner Up in the Daily Telegraphy/Arvon Competition 2000 www.helenclare.co.uk

A C Clarke is based in Glasgow. Her latest collections are *A Natural Curiosity,* (New Voices Press), shortlisted for the 2012 Callum Macdonald Award, and *Fr Meslier's Confession* (Oversteps Books). She was one of 17 poets commissioned to write a poem for the Mirrorball Commonwealth Poetry Anthology *The Laws of the Game* and is currently working on a fourth collection.

Jeff Cloves is a pop poet hack self-publisher.

Nick Cooke lives and works in London as a teacher of English as a Foreign Language. In addition to his poems, some of which have been published in Sentinel Literary Quarterly and Dream Catcher, he writes novels, plays, film scripts, and occasional literary criticism. In 2004 he published an article on John Updike in the quarterly Arete, edited by Craig Raine. He is also a music enthusiast and from 2006 to 2010 was the songwriter, vocalist and rhythm guitarist in a post-punk band called Live Wires.

Rachael Clyne lives in Glastonbury. She has been published in The Stare's Nest, IMPpress, Nutshells 'n Nuggetts, Domestic Cherry and the anthologies *The Listening Walk, The Book of Love and Loss.* Two collections *She Who Walks With Stones and Sings, Singing at the Bone Tree* are published by Indigo Dreams. In 2013 she won the Geoff Stevens Memorial prize. www.rachaelclyne.com

Richard Copeland has been writing on and off for about thirty years and has been published in various poetry magazines, including Envoi, The Black Mountain Review (Northern Ireland, sadly now defunct) and The Frogmore Papers. He is the Poetry Society's Stanza Rep for North Hertfordshire (Poetry ID).

Anthony Costello is a poet, writer and translator. His first book of poems, The Mask, was published by Lapwing in 2014. The Poems of Alain-Fournier, a collaborative translation project with Anita Marsh and Anthony Howell, is forthcoming in 2015 with Anvil Press.

Anna Crowe. Poet, translator of Catalan and Mexican poetry, she is co-founder and former Artistic Director of StAnza, Scotland's International Poetry Festival. Peterloo published two full collections, and her Mariscat collection, *Figure in a Landscape*, won the Callum Macdonald Memorial Award and was a Poetry Book Society Choice. Her latest book of translations, *Peatlands*, features the work of the Mexican poet, Pedro Serrano (Arc 2014). In 2005 she received a Travelling Scholarship from the Society of Authors.

Caroline Davies's first collection Convoy was published by Cinnamon Press in 2013. She was born in Norfolk to Welsh parents and spent much of her childhood by the sea. *Convoy* was inspired by the experiences of her grandfather, James 'Jim' Honeybill, who served on the Blue Funnel Line ship M.V. Ajax during the Malta convoys and also by her mother's stories of growing up in North Wales. She blogs occasionally at http://advancingpoetry.blogspot.com/

Celia Dixie is a member of the Sussex-based Green Room Poets. For many years she has met up regularly with two novelist friends to write together and spur each other on.

Spencer Edgar has always enjoyed writing poetry. His first book, White Orchid, is a collection stretching back 14 years capturing rites of passage where love is lost and found. When not contemplating grand design he works as a healthcare professional in the NHS. He lives with his partner and three children in Stroud in Gloucestershire.

Roger Elkin has won 45 First Prizes and several awards internationally, including the *Sylvia Plath Award for Poems about Women*, and the *Howard Sergeant Memorial Award for Services to Poetry* (1987*)*. His 11 collections include *Fixing Things* (2012); *Marking Time* (2012); *Bird in the Hand* (2012); *Chance Meetings* (2014). Editor of *Envoi*, (1991-2006), he is available for readings, workshops and poetry competition adjudication.

Martin Elster, author of *There's a Dog in the Heavens!*, is also a composer and serves as percussionist for the Hartford Symphony Orchestra. His poems have appeared in *Astropoetica, The Flea, The Martian Wave, The Rotary Dial,* and the anthologies *Taking Turns: Sonnets from Eratosphere, The 2012 Rhysling Anthology, and New Sun Rising: Stories for Japan.*

Martin's poem, "Walking With the Birds and the Bones Through Fairview Cemetery" received first place in the Thomas Gray Anniversary Poetry Competition 2014, and "Talcott Mountain" was nominated for a Pushcart Prize by *The Chimaera*.

Ututu Emmanuel is a Nigerian poet. He is an enthusiastic reader and has also writes short stories. He is currently a student of the Federal University of Technology Minna, Niger State, Nigeria.

Joe Fearn is a graduate of Hull University and The University of Leicester. He was shortlisted for the Smith/Doorstop poetry book prize in 2013. He lives and works in Hull.

Rachel J Fenton was born in the UK in 1976 and currently lives in New Zealand. Her poems have been shortlisted for numerous prizes, including the Royal Society of New Zealand Manhire Prize for Science Writing. AKA Rae Joyce, she is an AUT award winning graphic poet and is currently participating in the NZ Book Council's Graphic Novelist Exchange Residency with Taiwan in association with PANZ and TIBE, and is a registered mentor with the NZ Society of Authors. She blogs at snowlikethought.blogspot.co.nz

John Freeman's most recent collection is *White Wings: New and Selected Prose Poems* (Contraband, 2014). Others include *A Suite for Summer* (Worple), and *The Light Is Of Love, I Think: New and Selected Poems* (Stride). He taught for many years at Cardiff University. Website: http://www.johnfreemanpoetry.co.uk

Kate Firth. Previously an actress, Kate Firth's first pamphlet, Venus Reborn was published in 2013 by Chrysalis. She has performed at The Cheltenham and Bristol Poetry Festivals. She has also been published in three anthologies: Lacuna, In Protest (100 Poems for Human Rights) and a Star in the Heart. She is also voice coach for actors, broadcasters and in the non-profit and business sectors. She also runs performance skills workshops for poets, including the Winchester Poetry Festival.

Caron Freeborn used to write novels (*Three Blind Mice*, Abacus 2001 and *Prohibitions*, Abacus 2004), but after one of her children was diagnosed with Autism Spectrum Disorder, all words stopped together. When eventually the words came slithering back, she was amazed to find they were no longer prose, but poetry. Her first poetry collection, *Georges Perec is my hero,* is published by Circaidy Gregory Press, 2015.

Rose Flint is a writer and artist. She works as a poet in healthcare, in both communities and hospitals, taking poetry into many different wards and units. She won both the Cardiff and the Petra Kenney International Poetry Competition in 2008 and other awards include two Poetry Places. Her fifth collection, *A Prism for the Sun,* is published by Oversteps.

Margie Gaffron has written and published a volume of poetry (Holdings) and her work has appeared in a variety of magazines including The Progressive, Friends Journal, and Pivot. She has given poetry workshops and read her work in a variety of bookstores, coffee shops and college campuses. In 2012 she initiated the Fourth Friday Poetry Series at the Green Drake Art Center in Millheim, Pa. This series features readings by local writers as well as poets from outside the immediate area.

Charlotte Gann is a freelance writer and editor from Sussex. Her poetry pamphlet, *The Long Woman* (Pighog), was shortlisted for the 2012 Michael Marks Award.

Frances Gapper's flash fiction booklet *The Tiny Key* was published in 2009 by Sylph Editions and *Absent Kisses,* a story collection, in 2002 by Diva Books. She has stories in two issues of *Short Fiction* (University of Plymouth Press), in the Summer 2013 issue of Ireland-based magazine *The Moth* and in the *London Magazine* online. Her tiny story *Bluebeard's Daughter* won a competition run jointly by Creative Industries Trafford and the Manchester Literature Festival in autumn 2013. Other flashes appear in an anthology published in 2014 by Illinois-based *Twelve Winters* and in the *Reader's Digest*.

Vanessa Gebbie is a novelist, poet, short fiction writer, editor and freelance creative writing tutor. Her poetry has won the Troubadour and Sussex Poets competitions, and her pamphlet The Half-life of Fathers (Pighog) was selected by the TLS among the best of 2014. She is recipient of an Arts Council Grant for the Arts for her writing, a

Hawthornden International Fellowship and a Gladstone's Library Residency. www.vanessagebbie.com

Caroline Gill's poetry chapbook, *The Holy Place*, co-authored with John Dotson, was published by The Seventh Quarry (Swansea) in conjunction with Cross-Cultural Communications (New York) in 2012. Caroline has won several prizes, including the international Petra Kenney Poetry Competition (General Section) in 2007 and the debut Zoological Society of London (ZSL) Poetry Competition in 2013. Three poems were included in *The Book of Forms: A Handbook of Poetics, Including Odd and Invented Forms* by Lewis Putnam Turco (UPNE 2011). Website: **www.carolinegillpoetry.com**

Kay Green is the administrator of Earlyworks Press, a club for writers and illustrators, best known for its poetry and fiction competitions. She was formerly an English teacher and has also been a writer of fantasy fiction for most of her adult life. Her first story collection, 'Jung's People' was published by Elastic Press in 2004, and later re-released by her own Circaidy Gregory Press after she strayed into small press publishing. Her poetry, stories and articles have appeared in a range of magazines and collections.

Jan Harris lives in Nottinghamshire and writes poetry, flash fiction and short stories. Her work has appeared in *14 Magazine, nth Position, Popshot, Mslexia* and other places.

Marc Harshman's full-length poetry collection, GREEN-SILVER AND SILENT was published by Bottom Dog, OH in 2012 and four chapbooks include ROSE OF SHARON, Mad River, MA. Periodical publications: *The Georgia Review, The Progressive, Appalachian Heritage, Poetry Salzburg Review, Emerson Review,* and *Shenandoah*. Poems anthologized: Kent State University, the University of Iowa, University of Georgia, and the University of Arizona. Eleven children's books have been published and three more titles are forthcoming.

Mark Haworth-Booth is the author of *Wild Track: poems with pictures by friends* (2006). He is a Green Party activist and lives in North Devon.

Tania Hershman is the author of two story collections: *My Mother Was An Upright Piano: Fictions* (Tangent Books, 2012), and *The White Road and Other Stories* (Salt, 2008). Tania's poetry has been published in Magma, Butcher's Dog, Obsessed with Pipework, Poems in Which and Amaryllis. Tania is founder and curator of ShortStops (www.shortstops.info), celebrating short story activity across the UK & Ireland and is studying for a PhD in Creative Writing at Bath Spa University. She is co-writer and editor of Writing Short Stories: A Writers' & Artists' Companion (Bloomsbury, Dec 2014). www.taniahershman.com

Alison Hill has published two collections, Peppercorn Rent (Flarestack, 2008) and Slate Rising (Indigo Dreams, 2014) and is currently working on a third. She founded and runs Rhythm & Muse and was Kingston Libraries' first Poet in Residence. She also writes plays and flash fiction.

Norbert Hirschhorn is a public health physician, commended by President Bill Clinton as an "American Health Hero." He lives in London and Beirut. He has published four collections: *A Cracked River* (Slow Dancer Press, London, 1999), *Mourning in the Presence of a Corpse* (Dar al-Jadeed, Beirut, 2008), *Monastery of the Moon* (Dar al-Jadeed, Beirut, 2012), and *To Sing Away the Darkest Days. Poems Re-imagined from Yiddish Folksongs* (Holland Park Press, London, 2013). His poems have appeared in numerous US/UK publications, several as prize-winning. Website: www.bertzpoet.com.

Bill Holdsworth was born London 1929. He is a professional engineer who has balanced architectural and city planing climatic adaptive engineering solutions with community politics and the arts. He kick-started the 1960's UK-wide arts movement CENTRE 42 and brought playwright Arnold on board. He has led a long eclectic life as a world-wide lecturer, a writer, poet and journalist and is a travelling man.

Penny Hope is a teacher based in Sussex. She has poems published in a variety of magazines, and is a member of the Green Room Poets.

Neil Howell has recently retired after many years in the IT industry and is now focussing his attention and experience on community projects and change. He has also had a long interest in poetry and with the time now have available has been writing some poems himself. In 2013 he came up with a way of combining these two interests. He decided to take a news headline from each day and write something about it in verse. The result was a fascinating picture of 'change' through the year.

Georgi Y. Johnson. Spiritual teacher and author Georgi Y. Johnson was born in Sheffield in 1967. After graduating in English Literature from Oxford, she moved to Israel where she now lives with her partner Bart and her seven children. Georgi teaches worldwide on nonduality, awakening and perception. She is author of: I AM HERE - Opening the Windows to Life & Beauty, a book inquiring into consciousness, awareness and emptiness as forms of perception.

Strider Marcus Jones – a poet, law graduate and ex civil servant from Salford, England with proud Celtic roots in Ireland and Wales. A member of The Poetry Society, his five published books of poetry are modern, traditional, mythical, sometimes romantic, surreal and metaphysical. His poetry has been published in over forty publications including: A New Ulster Magazine; The Screech Owl; Degenerates Voices For Peace Anthology; The Huffington Post USA; mgv2 Publishing Anthology; Deep Water Literary Journal; The Stray Branch Literary Magazine; East Coast Literary Review and Crack The Spine Literary Magazine. https://stridermarcusjonespoetry.wordpress.com/is

Oonah V Joslin is current poetry editor at The Linnet's Wings. She lives in Northumberland, England.

Siham Karami co-owns a technology recycling company and lives in Florida, USA. Her poetry has been or will be published in *Measure, Unsplendid, String Poet, Angle Poetry, Postcard Poetry and Prose, Kin Poetry Journal, The Amsterdam Quarterly, Shot Glass Journal, Snakeskin, Innisfree Journal,* and *The Centrifugal Eye,* among other places. She is a Pushcart Prize nominee, and has won the Laureates' Prize in the Maria W. Faust sonnet contest.

Wendy Klein is US born but has lived in the UK most of her adult life. A retired family therapist and family mediator, she is published in many magazines and journals including *Mslexia, The North, Smiths Knoll, The Interpreter's House, Artemis, Oxford Poetry, Seam,* and *The*

South. Winner of the Buxton, the Havant and the 'Sonnet or Not' Poetry competitions in 2014, she is published in many anthologies, including *The Book of Love and Loss* and the forthcoming *Raving Beauties*.

Desmond Kon Zhicheng-Mingdé is the author of the epistolary novel, *Singular Acts of Endearment*, as well as three poetry collections. Founding editor of Squircle Line Press, Desmond has edited over fifteen books and co-produced three audio books. His honors include the PEN American Center Shorts Prize, Swale Life Poetry Prize, Notre Dame Poetry Fellowship, NAC Creation Grant, Gardens-by-the-Bay Residency, Singapore International Foundation Grant, and Little Red Tree Poetry Prize, among other awards.

Camilla Lambert has had poems published in 'SOUTH', 'Interpreter's House', 'Sentinel Literary Quarterly and 'Poetry Cornwall', also in several anthologies. A number have been placed or highly commended in competitions. She co-edited an anthology of poems 'Island Voices' (2010). In 2012 she gained an Open University First Class Honours degree in Literature with Creative Writing. Her first pamphlet is to be published by Indigo Dreams Publishing towards the end of 2015.

Martha Landman. South African born poet Martha Landman lives in North Queensland, Australia where she practices as a psychologist. She has been supporting the work of *Medicins Sans Frontieres* for many years. Her work has appeared in various online journals and anthologies, including *Mused, Camel Saloon, New Verse News, Jellyfish Whispers, Eunoia Review* and *Blood on the Floor.*

Andie Lewenstein's poems are published in Scintilla, Cinnamon Press, Blinking eye, Obsessed With Pipework, Poetry South East, Artemis and Railroad Poetry. She was co-director of the Poetry OtherWise conference in Sussex.

Lin Lundie lives and writes on the South Coast and writes a poetry diary. She is a textile artist, and her special interests are antique lace and interior design. She runs a poetry group, 'The River Poets', in Arundel, West Sussex.

Christina Lloyd. Born in Hong Kong, raised in the Philippines and educated in the United States, Christina Lloyd holds an MA in Hispanic languages and literatures from U.C. Berkeley, and an MA in creative writing from Lancaster University. In addition to a couple of pamphlets published in the States, her work appears in various journals, The North among them.

Alison Lock is a writer of short stories and poetry. Her first collection, A Slither of Air was published in 2011; a short story collection, Above the Parapet, in 2013; and a forthcoming poetry collection, Beyond Wings, 2015. Her work is published in many journals and anthologies - including her competition winning stories in Sentinel Champions. www.alisonlock.com

Rupert Loydell is Senior Lecturer in English with Creative Writing at Falmouth University the editor of Stride magazine, and a Contributing Editor to International Times. His many books of poetry include The Return Of The Man Who Has Everything (Shearsman 2015) and Ballads of the Alone (Shearsman 2013).

Lennart Lundh is a poet, short-fictionist, historian, and photographer. His work has appeared internationally since 1965. Len and his wife, Lin, live near Chicago.

Anna Lunt has written poems as a personal journal for a number of years. In 2014, her husband Anthony, who is a psychotherapist, asked her to publish her anthology *Poems of the Infinite and Eternal* as a companion volume to his book *Avision – The Way of the Dream*. Anna and Anthony have five children.

Linus Łyszkowska, who was born in Scotland in 1926, grew up in Bridge of Allan, Stirlingshire. She and her Polish husband, Marian, lived for many happy years in Brazil. Now widowed, she has been living in Cambridge since 2000. She began to write poetry in 2009.

Caroline Maldonado lives in London and Italy. Her poems have been accepted in a wide range of magazines including Iota, Orbis, Tears in the Fence and Agenda, as well as in anthologies and online. Poetry publications include *What they say in Avenale* (Indigo Dreams Publishing 2014) and a co-translation from Italian of the poetry of

Rocco Scotellaro, *Your call keeps us awake*, published by Smokestack Books (May 2013).

Alwyn Marriage's poetry is widely published in magazines and anthologies, and three of her seven published books have been poetry. She has won and been placed in a number of competitions, and held Poet in Residence posts with Ballet Rambert and with the Winchester Arts Festival. She is Managing Editor of Oversteps Books, holds a research fellowship at the University of Surrey, and gives readings all over Britain and abroad. Previously she has been a university lecturer, chief executive of two NGOs, a Rockefeller International Scholar and Editor of a journal.

Paul Matthews, poet, teacher and gymnast has taught for many years at Emerson College. He is renowned for helping poets and writers, even the most anxious, to work with and develop their creative voice. His inspiring books, Sing Me the Creation, and Words in Place (both from Hawthorn Press) contain numerous exercises to nurture the creative process and bring language alive between people. The Ground that Love Seeks and Slippery Characters (Five Seasons Press) are gatherings of his poetry. See www.paulmatthewspoetry.co.uk

Pansy Maurer-Alvarez was born in Puerto Rico, did her literary studies at universities in the US, Switzerland and Spain and now lives and writes in France. Her work has appeared in numerous publications across Europe and the US and in several anthologies. Some poems have been translated into French, German and Spanish. Her latest poetry collection is *In a Form of Suspension* (corrupt press, Paris, 2014) and she has 4 previous collections. She is a contributing editor to the British magazine, *Tears in the Fence* and curates the monthly reading series *Poets Live* in Paris.

John McCullough's first collection of poems The Frost Fairs (Salt, 2011) won the Polari First Book Prize. It was a Book of the Year for The Independent and The Poetry School, and a summer read for The Observer. He lives in Hove.

Gill McEvoy runs regular, and occasional, poetry events in Chester. Two collections have been published by Cinnamon Press: "The Plucking Shed" 2010, "Rise", 2013. Her third pamphlet from

Happenstance Press, "The First Telling", has just been published. She is a Hawthornden Fellow.

Jehanne Mehta is a singer-songwriter and poet, who writes performs and records songs and poems for the Earth Soul and Spirit.Website www.jehannemehta.com

Diana Mitchener (M.A. Creative Writing, 2000) is an active participant in poetry workshops in West Sussex . She published 'Ten Poems for Performance' and a further selection of her poems in 'Corncockle' in 2009. 'Holding the Line - a life' (Leaf Books, 2011) recreates the experiences of war-time evacuation in Shropshire and traces its life-long effects. www.corncockle.co.uk

Helen Moore is an award-winning ecopoet. Her debut collection, *Hedge Fund, And Other Living Margins* (Shearsman Books, 2012) will be followed by *ECOZOA*, described by John Kinsella as "a milestone in the journey of ecopoetics". It will be published by Permanent Publications in March 2015.

Mary E. Moore is a retired physician who began seriously writing poetry after her retirement from a career in Rheumatology. Her poems have been widely published and a selection can be seen on her website, http://www.maryemoorepoetry.com

Kyle Norwood is the winner of the 2014 Morton Marr Poetry Prize from Southwest Review. His poems have also appeared or will soon appear in Innisfree Poetry Journal, Right Hand Pointing, Seneca Review, and elsewhere. After earning a doctorate in English at UCLA, he taught for many years in the public high school system in Los Angeles, where he still lives.

Chris O'Carroll is a writer and an actor. His poems have appeared in *14 by 14, Life and Legends, Light, Measure, The New Verse News*, and *Umbrella*, among other print and online journals, and in the anthologies *The Best of the Barefoot Muse* and *20 Years at the Cantab Lounge*.

Dr Tunde Oseni bagged a First Class Honours degree in Political Science from Nigeria's premier University of Ibadan, where he was a MacArthur Foundation scholar at the University of Ghana, Legon in

2005. He earned an MSc at the prestigious University of Oxford, United Kingdom, and Doctorate and at the University of Exeter, where he taught for three years. He is currently a University Lecturer and Consultant in Nigeria.

Patrick B. Osada works as an editor, writes reviews of poetry for magazines and is a member of the Management Team for **SOUTH** Poetry Magazine. His first collection, *Close to the Edge* was published in 1996 & won the prestigious *Rosemary Arthur Award.* His second collection, *Short Stories : Suburban Lives* and his last volume, *Rough Music,* have been published in England by *Bluechrome.* His current collection, *Choosing the Route,* has been published in England by *Indigo Dreams Publishing.* His website is www.poetry-patrickosada.co.uk

Irena Pasvinter divides her time between software engineering, endless family duties and writing poetry and fiction. Her stories and poems have appeared in online magazines (Every Day Poets, Every Day Fiction, Madswirl, Camroc Press, Fiction 365, Rose & Thorn and others) and in Poetry Quarterly. She is currently working on her never-ending first novel.

Mario Petrucci is a PhD physicist and ecologist intensely active at the literature-ecology-science membrane, generating groundbreaking educational resources and poetry that meets issues of searing social, linguistic and personal relevance with innovation and humanity. Mario Petrucci's work aspires to "Poetry on a geological scale" (*Verse*). *Heavy Water: a poem for Chernobyl* (Enitharmon, 2004) secured the Daily Telegraph/ Arvon Prize and "inflicts... the finest sort of shock... to the conscience, to the soul" (*Poetry London*). *i tulips* (Enitharmon, 2010) takes its name from his vast Anglo-American sequence of 1111 poems, hailed by the Poetry Book Society as "modernist marvels".

Jay Ramsay is the author of 35 books of poetry, non-fiction, and classic Chinese translation with Martin Palmer. His latest publications are *Agistri Notebook* (KFS, 2014), *Monuments* (Waterloo Press, 2014), and *Shu Jing—the Book of History* (Penguin Classics, 2014). He is also poetry editor of *Caduceus* magazine, and works in private practice as a UKCP accredited psychotherapist and healer, also running personal development workshops worldwide (www.jayramsay.co.uk.)

Susan Richardson is a poet, performer and educator, with two collections, *Creatures of the Intertidal Zone* and *Where the Air is Rarefied*, from Cinnamon Press. Her third collection, *skindancing*, themed around human-animal metamorphosis and exploring our dys/functional relationship with the wild, will be published in 2015. She has performed at literary, environmental and science festivals throughout the UK, for organisations such as WWF and Friends of the Earth, on BBC 2, Radio 4 and at Universities both nationally and internationally. www.susanrichardsonwriter.co.uk

Michaela Ridgway lives in Brighton. Her magazine credits include Magma, Orbis, Other Poetry, The Frogmore Papers, Tears in the Fence, Antiphon and The Interpreter's House. She hosts the monthly Pighog Plus! Poetry night in Brighton, UK (http://www.pighog.co.uk).

Miles Salter lives in York, and enjoys being a writer, musician and storyteller. His poetry collections include 'The Border' (Valley Press, 2011) and 'Animals' (Valley Press, 2013). He is Visiting Lecturer at Leeds Trinity University and Director of York Literature Festival. He finds spiders difficult.

Robert Schechter has published poems and translations in *Highlights for Children, High Five, The Washington Post, The Evansville Review, String Poet, Poetry East, The Alabama Literary Review, Light Quarterly,* and *Lighten Up Online,* among other journals, and in various anthologies.

Jean-Mark Sens was born in France and educated in Paris. He has lived in the American South for over twenty years, and dwells "poetically" in New Orleans. He teaches culinary arts at Mississippi University for Women in Gulfport, MS, delving on a daily basis in the tensions between nature and culture, the raw and the cook, and other philosophical matters often encountered in a kitchen. He has published poems in magazines in the U.S. and Canada, and a first collection, *Appetite*, with Red Hen Press:

Gordon Simms. Formally head of Performing Arts at what is now Blackburn University, Gordon hoped for a quiet life on retiring to rural France in 2002. However, in 2012 he organised the first Bilingual LitFest in the tiny village of St Clémentin. In 2014 the festival was repeated gaining EU recognition and funding. A third is planned for 2016 in tandem with festivals in Italy, Spain and the UK. As well as writing poetry Gordon thoroughly enjoys playwriting and is currently involved with a newly founded theatre company for whom he is directing. His collected poems, *Uphill to the Sea*, won the Biscuit prize, 2012. simms.gordon@orange.fr   www.stclementinlitfest.com

Jocelyn Simms is organiser of the Segora International Writing Competitions launched in 2007. Currently she is writing a sequence of poems tracing the development and testing of the atomic bomb, hoping that looking back to the momentous events of 1945 might inform current debate. She was delighted to welcome Blake Morrison and Michèle Roberts as principal guests at the bilingual LitFest in 2014 and as judges of the Segora poetry and short story competitions of that year. jocelynsmms@gmail.com   www.poetryproseandplays.com

Wendy Sloan's work has appeared or is forthcoming in various journals including *Big City Lit, Blue Unicorn, Light, Measure, Mezzo Cammin, TheRaintown Review, Think Journal,* and *Umbrella Journal.* Her translations (Leopardi/Stampa) have been published or are forthcoming in *The Able Muse, The Chimaera,* and *Measure.*Sloan was a finalist in the Howard Nemerov Sonnet Competition (2006) and has been nominated for a Pushcart Prize. She co-hosts the Carmine Street Metrics reading series in New York City.

Beth Somerford's poetry ranges from the intimate and personal, to the sweep of landscape poems. It draws particularly on science and social history, a fascination with place and a love of the mundane. Her poems have been published in Magma, Equinox, Obsessed with Pipework, Orbis, Iota, The Cannon's Mouth and the French Literary Review.Beth lives in Brighton with her composer husband and an ever shifting number of children. As well as writing, she coaches, acts and directs, runs workshops, pots and potters about.

K.V.Skene's work has appeared in Canadian, U.K., U.S., Irish, Australian and Austrian magazines, most recently in *Poetry Cornwall, The Maynard* (Canada), *Contemporary Literary Review India, The Saving Bannister* (Canada), *The Stony Thursday Book* (Ireland) and *Obsessed With Pipework.* Her publications include *Love in the (Irrational) Imperfect,* 2006, Hidden Brook Press (Canada) and *You Can Almost Hear Their Voices,* 2010, Indigo Dreams Publications (UK). She placed third in the Cardiff International Poetry Competition 2014 and currently lives and writes from Toronto, Canada.

Richard Skinner's poems have been published in HARK, The Interpreter's House and Magma and longlisted for the National Poetry Competition. His full collection, 'the light user scheme', is published by Smokestack. His new pamphlet, 'Terrace' (Smokestack), is published in April 2015.

Susan Skinner has had four collections of her poems published: Monet's Garden - Headland Press, The Minnow Catching Boys - Headland Press, Island Sisters - Redlake Press, Out of Nowhere - Searle Publishing. She has also published in poetry magazines, and has published stories for children, and illustrated and compiled three Christian books: Secret Journey - John Hunt Publishing; Graces for Today - John Hunt Publishing; Symbols of the Soul - John Hunt Publishing.

Thomas R. Smith is the author of seven published books of poems, most recently THE GLORY (2015, Red Dragonfly Press). He has also edited several books, including AIRMAIL: THE LETTERS OF ROBERT BLY AND TOMAS TRANSTRÖMER (Bloodaxe, 2013). He lives in western Wisconsin and teaches poetry at the Loft Literary Center in Minneapolis. His work has appeared in several publications in the UK and Ireland.

Anne Stewart runs the online showcase www.poetrypf.co.uk and is Administrator for Second Light, a network of women poets. Her awards include the Bridport Prize (2008) and the Silver Wyvern (Italy, 2014). Her first collection, *The Janus Hour,* was published by Oversteps Books in 2010.

Seán Street has published nine collections, the most recent being *Cello* (Rockingham Press, 2013) and *Jazz Time* (Lapwing Publications, 2014). Prose includes *The Dymock Poets* (Seren 1994/2014), *The Poetry of Radio: The Colour of Sound* (Routledge, 2013) and *The Memory of Sound: Preserving the Sonic Past* (Routledge, 2014). He is Emeritus Professor at Bournemouth University.

Susan Taylor has six published poetry collections, the most recent of which is *A Small Wave for Your Form* from Oversteps Books in 2012. She coedits the South West poetry journal *The Broadsheet* with her partner, Simon Williams.

Eilidh Thomas lives in north east Scotland with her husband and collie dog, Smudge. She writes poetry and short stories, which have been published, selectively, in print and online over the past few years. Recent work is published in Sentinel Literary Quarterly and The Stare's Nest.

Mark Totterdell's poems have appeared in many magazines and have won competitions. His first collection, 'This Patter of Traces',was published in 2014 by Oversteps Books.

Clare Whistler is a collaborative, site -specific artist, who makes events using many art forms with all sorts of people. www.clarewhistler.co.uk

Simon Williams has written poetry for 40 years, starting at university. *A Place Where Odd Animals Stand* (Oversteps Books, 2012) is his fourth independently published collection and *He/She* (Itinerant Press, 2013) his fifth. Simon makes a living as a technology journalist and lives in a cottage on the southern edge of Dartmoor with his wife, poet Susan Taylor. He has two sons and, so far, three grandchildren.

Jackie Wills' most recent collections of poetry are *Woman's Head as Jug* (Arc, 2013) and *Commandments* (Arc, 2007). She was shortlisted for the 1995 TS Eliot prize for her first collection. In 2004 she was one of Mslexia magazine's 10 new women poets of the decade. Wills has earned her living as a writer since 1978.

Margaret Wilmot. Born in California, Margaret Wilmot has lived in Sussex since 1978. She is drawn by imaginative associations . . . memory, landscape, ideas, paintings, words – seeing where the pencil leads. A pamphlet has been published by Smiths Knoll entitled *Sweet Coffee*.

Matthew Wilson, 31, has had over 150 appearances in such places as *Horror Zine, Star*Line, Spellbound, Illumen, Apokrupha Press, Hazardous Press, Gaslight Press, Sorcerers Signal* and many more. He is currently editing his first novel and can be contacted on twitter @matthew94544267.

Marc Woodward was born in the USA but lives in rural England where he combines playing music, writing and occasional tv presenting. He has been published in a number of magazines and has had work included in anthologies from Ravenshead Press, Forward Press and others. He has been featured on the websites of the Poetry Society and The Guardian. More of his work can be seen on his blog http://marcwoodwardpoetry.blogspot.co.uk

Shirley Wright is a Bristol-based novelist and widely published poet. Her poetry collection "The Last Green Field", published by Indigo Dreams, came out in September 2013.

Jacquie Wyatt. After a lucky escape from a big brand marketing career Jacquie Wyatt is a poet. Too often distracted by flash fiction, stories and five novels to date her razor sharp brain deduced that putting everything in a very deep drawer wasn't helping. A frequent Write Invite winner and runner-up she was a Flash flood author in 2012. She is a founder member of Roundel – the Tonbridge Poetry stanza.

Dr. Aprilia Zank is a lecturer for Creative Writing and Translation in the Department of Languages and Communication at the Ludwig Maximilian University of Munich, Germany. She is also a poet, a translator and the editor of the English–German anthology *poetry tREnD Eine englisch-deutsche Anthologie zeitgenössischer Lyrik*, LIT Verlag, Berlin, 2010, and the anthology *POETS IN PERSON at the Glassblower* (Indigo Dream Publishing, April, 2014). Her poetry collection, *TERMINUS ARCADIA*, was 2nd Place Winner at the Twowolvz Press Poetry Chapbook Contest 2013. She is also a passionate photographer.

Simon Zonenblick. A poet living in the Ryburn Valley, Yorkshire Simon works mainly in libraries and dabbles in gardening. Two collections of his poetry have been published: *Little Creatures* -poems of Insects, Small Mammals and Micro-organisms (Caterpillar Poetry) & *Random Journeys* (Unpretentious Arts).

Afterword

With every injury, with every illness, with every trauma, lived through on account of age, accident, conflict or war, the human spirit stands at the threshold of a new way of being. Physical and emotional challenges presenting such transforming forces do not limit themselves to any gender, age, or geographic demarcation. It makes sense that the brave and selfless egos who wrestle these challenges believe in our common humanity, come from everywhere and work everywhere...without borders.

Born in the Republic of Biafra six days after the first shots of the Nigeria-Biafra war were fired, I was excited when *All the Invisibles* author and *Sentinel Literary Quarterly* Editor, Mandy Pannett suggested *Poems for a Liminal Age* to support Médecins Sans Frontières (MSF). I was excited because, as the Psalmist wrote; "Weeping may endure for a night, but joy cometh in the morning" it was comforting to me that the war and famine in Biafra, the country of my birth, that carnage that lasted three years, was one of the key triggers that led to the formation of MSF – a joy that came in 1971 and continues to grow and grow. Let's call that the silver lining.

Poems for a Liminal Age is dedicated to the over 30,000 MSF staff and volunteers working all over the world, redefining emergency medical aid... saving lives. MSF workers stand without fear wherever there is conflict, injury and sickness. That is why so many poets have put their words where their hearts are. This book marks a coming together of inspired words to say thank you and to say keep up the excellent and humbling work you do.

Poems for a Liminal Age also celebrates the visionary founders of MSF:

> Dr Jacques Beres,
> Philippe Bernier,

Raymond Borel,
Dr Jean Cabrol
Dr Marcel Delcourt,
Dr Xavier Emmanuelli
Dr Pascal Greletty-Bosviel,
Gérard Illiouz
Dr Bernard Kouchner,
Dr Gérard Pigeon
Vladan Radoman,
Dr Max Recamier,
Dr Jean-Michel Wild

Many profound words have been written through the ages on just about every possible human experience. Every piece of writing captures a moment and releases it into the ether for generations to come. In *Poems for a Liminal Age* we encounter one hundred and ninety-nine such moments of physical, emotional, and spiritual unfoldment, given freely by so many amazing poets to support a worthy organization and her cause. It is a fact of natural law that the pens of all contributors to this book will never lack ink, but not theirs only, but also the pens of the hundreds of poets who submitted their poems but whose works could not be included in this volume, mostly due to space constraints. Thank you all.

It is our hope that this book will be well-promoted by all and well-received across the world so that we can do as much as we can for MSF. The amount of money and other gifts or resources MSF requires to do the great work they do is not something that can be funded by a poetry book, but whatever we can raise with this book will help in some way to make somebody's life better, somewhere in the world.

Nnorom Azuonye
publisher@spmpublications.com

Lightning Source UK Ltd.
Milton Keynes UK
UKOW02f0321260815

257499UK00003B/130/P